Norwich Historic Homes & Families

Researched and written by

MARIAN K. O'KEEFE AND CATHERINE SMITH DOROSHEVICH

Consultant Editor	*Photography by*
PHILIP A. JOHNSON	MARIAN K. O'KEEFE

Published in cooperation with

THE SOCIETY OF THE FOUNDERS OF NORWICH

The PEQUOT  PRESS, Inc.

STONINGTON   CONNECTICUT

Dedicated to
TIM and PETER

ERRATA

Page iv, 8 Vergason Ave. *Loomer* Family (not Loomis)

Page v, Parmenas Jones. Built prior to *1800*

Page viii, *205* Gifford Street (not 204)

Page 60, gift (not bequest)

Page 68, 1861 (not 1871)

Page 83, gift (not bequest)

Page 101, 205 Gifford *Street,* East Great Plain

Page 108, Taftville. There *is* some textile manufacturing done here.

Acknowledgments

We are deeply indebted to many persons who have inspired, guided and helped in the putting together of this book. Our gratitude is especially due to the owners and caretakers of the properties described and photographed.

Many people helped our search for the information on which the book is based. Of these, we particularly acknowledge the assistance of the following:

Mrs. S. Pearce Browning III
Mr. Raymond Case
Mrs. Ada R. Chase
Mr. Elmer Farnham
Mr. Carl Feiss, F.O.I.A., A.I.P.,
    National Trust for Historic
    Preservation
Mrs. Clifford Harvey

Mrs. Myra Linton
Mrs. Edward Little
Mrs. Antranig Papelian
Mrs. Frank Roethel
Mr. Richard Sharpe, A.I.A.
Mrs. A. Robert Schnip
Miss Mary Wildowsky

We are also grateful to the following sources of information and to the staffs of each for their unstinting help in checking facts:

Otis Library, Norwich

The Antiquarian & Landmarks Society of Connecticut, Hartford

Norton-Peck Library of the Norwich Free Academy

Connecticut State Library, Hartford

Archives of the Society of the Founders of Norwich, Leffingwell Inn

The Norwich Bulletin

Special mention should be made of the extraordinary professional and technical services given to us by our forbearing Consultant Editor, Philip A. Johnson, by our publisher, the Pequot Press, and by Photo-Lab, Inc. for expert photographic processing work to produce prints of reproduction quality.

List of Norwich Houses Surveyed

Houses marked with an asterisk (*) are illustrated in this book.

Houses marked (HABS) are listed in the Historic American Building Survey in the Library of Congress. Washington, D. C.

YANTIC SECTION

Address	Original or Early Owner	Date Built
Willimantic Rd. (Formerly Yantic Village Rd.)	Waterman Family	Circa 1760

BEAN HILL SECTION

Address	Original or Early Owner	Date Built
8 Vergason Ave. (Formerly 4 Huntington Ave.	Loomis Family	Prior 1750
Huntington Ave.		
5	Hyde Family	Circa 1750
6	Huntington Family	Circa 1750
8	Fillmore Family	Circa 1750
45	Ebenezer Huntington	1717
46	Charles Avery	Circa 1752
Case Street		
21	David Waterman	Prior 1800
21R	John Leffingwell	Prior 1750
22	Birchard-Kearney	Prior 1800
32	Griswold Family	Prior 1800
32R	Old Cider Mill	1801
Sturtevant Street		
139	Richard Edgerton	1660-1750

NORWICHTOWN SECTION

Address	Original or Early Owner	Date Built
West Town Street		
8	Sterry Family	Prior 1830
14	Possibly Hyde Family	Prior 1800
17	Unknown	Prior 1800
18	Unknown	Prior 1800
21	John D. Perkins	Circa 1772

29	Dr. Philip Turner	Prior 1700
79	William Mansfield	Prior 1800
94	Benjamin Huntington	Circa 1760
122	Aaron Cleveland	Circa 1780
156	Billings Family	Circa 1760
199	Francis Gookin	Prior 1750
210	John Baldwin	1660-1750
215	Austin Family	Circa 1750
232	Hugh Caulkins	Prior 1790

East Town Street

19	Capt. Joshua Huntington	1738
23	Gen. Jedediah Huntington	1765
33	Unknown (Moved from Bean Hill)	Circa 1750
34	Gov. Samuel Huntington	1783
35	Jabez Perkins	1758
44	Joseph Trumbull	1763
47	Samuel Abbott	1752
51	Capt. William Whiting	1760
55	Gardner Carpenter (HABS)	1793
69	Daniel Lathrop School	1783
73	Joseph Carpenter (Silversmith) (HABS)	1772
77	Jesse Brown Tavern	1787-90
79	J. & C. P. Huntington Store	1801
81	Norwich Congregational Church	1801

Mediterranean Lane

8	Samuel Charlton	Prior 1800
12	Richard Charlton (HABS)	Prior 1757
14	Parmenas Jones	Prior 1700

Elm Avenue

2	Simon Huntington Jr. Tavern	1690
6	Curtis Cleveland	Prior 1733
8	Sarah Knight—Peck's Tavern	1698-1734
10	Sylvanus Jones	1734
14	William Morgan	1747-52

Huntington Lane

11	Col. Joshua Huntington	1771
16	Bradford-Huntington (HABS)	Prior 1691
30	Rev. Joseph Strong	1778

Scotland Road

25	Thomas Danforth	1746
155	Thomas Hughes	1753
276	Lathrop Family	Circa 1750
433	Lillibridge Family	Prior 1800

Ox Hill Road
10   Michael Darrow   1743-1773

Canterbury Turnpike
2   Samuel Avery—Major Tracy Store 1785
6   William Lathrop   1744

Town Street
2   David Greenleaf   1761
5   Capt. William Billings   1750
85   Samuel Manning   1750
86   Eleazer Lord Tavern   1760

Harland Road
5   Thomas Leffingwell 4th   1733-58
7   Samuel Leffingwell   Circa 1744
13   Daniel Leffingwell Stocking   Prior 1800
                Factory
20   James Lincoln   1784

Sachem Plains Road
9   Capt. Philemon Winship   Prior 1800

Washington Street
335   Lt. Thomas Leffingwell   1710
348   Stephen Backus (Leffingwell   1675
                Inn) (HABS)
357   Thomas Harland   1779
363   Thomas Williams   1759
365   East District School   Circa 1789
371   Simeon Case   1750
377   Dr. Joshua Lathrop (HABS)   1763
380   Thomas Lathrop   1660-1745
385   Thomas Lathrop   1783
387   Daniel Lathrop Coit   1785
407   Joshua Prior   1766
409   James Norman   Circa 1760
410   Christopher Huntington 2nd   Prior 1735
417   Felix Huntington   1771
420   Ezra Huntington   1771
425   Daniel Tracy   1785

CHELSEA PARADE SECTION

Crescent Street
108   Lafayette S. Foster   1853
108   Slater Memorial Museum (HABS) 1886

Chelsea Parade South
9   Joseph Teel (Hotel)   1789

vi

Rockwell Street
42	Joseph Perkins	1825
44	Nathaniel Backus	1750

Washington Street
154	J. Newton Perkins	1850
157	Ebenezer Learned (HABS)	1799
185	Charles A. Converse (HABS)	1870
268	William C. Gilman	1823
276	Capt. Jonathan Chester	1755-59

LITTLE PLAIN SECTION

Broadway
167	Woodhull Family (HABS)	Circa 1830
171	Johnson Family (HABS)	1840
181	Thomas Coit	Circa 1790
185	Hezekiah Perkins (HABS)	1775-1800
189	Capt. Jacob DeWitt (HABS)	1775-1800
231	Gen. William G. Ely (HABS)	Circa 1850

Slater Avenue
2	Slater Family	Circa 1850

Union Street
34	Unknown	Prior 1800
89	Francis Leavens	Prior 1840

Elmwood Avenue
18-20	Slater Family	1833
31	Slater Family	Circa 1850

DOWNTOWN SECTION

Cliff Street
158	Roath Family	1734-1785

Main Street
307	Gov. William A. Buckingham	1845
352	John F. Slater (HABS)	Circa 1827

Church Street
58	Unknown	Circa 1750
62	Rev. John Tyler	1768

Washington Street
23	Dr. Elijah S. Kinney	1780
92	Elijah Lathrop	1780
99	Jonathan Dodge (HABS)	1732
118	John Vernet (HABS)	1809

TAFTVILLE SECTION

Route 12 (Norwich Ave.)	Ponemah Mills Worker's House (HABS)	1871-1900
	Ponemah Mills (HABS)	1866-1871

WESTSIDE SECTION

Maple Street 24	Donahue-Woods (HABS)	Circa 1835

THAMESVILLE SECTION

West Thames Street 371	Richard Bushnell	Prior 1690

EAST GREAT PLAINS SECTION

Gifford Street		
45	Gifford Family	Prior 1800
147	Gifford Family	Prior 1800
204	John A. Gifford	1805
New London Turnpike		
Cor. Old Salem Rd.	Peter Morgan	Prior 1770
179 Salem Turnpike	Ellis Family	Prior 1800
346 Salem Turnpike	Beebe Family	Prior 1800
Manwaring Road	Manwaring Family	1793

TRADING COVE SECTION

New London Turnpike at Lucas Street	Maples Family (Red Tavern)	Prior 1735

OTHER NOTEWORTHY SITES

Yantic Bridge, Yantic, Conn. Built in 1908 for Winslow T. Williams.

Benedict Arnold Well, 299 Washington Street. (Arnold House gone.)

Little Plain Fountain, Broadway and Union Streets, erected by D. A. R.

Monument to U.S.S. Maine, Chelsea Parade.

Shannon Mausoleum, St. Mary's Cemetery, Greenville. Built in 1917 (HABS)

The
Economic
Background

A Brief Commercial and Industrial History
of Norwich, Connecticut

By Philip A. Johnson

Various cycles of prosperity and adversity are common to the life of a community and an individual. The economic background is mirrored in the houses and other buildings erected from time to time. In studying the houses of Old Norwich an orderly delineation of the successive changes in economic conditions provides an interesting commentary on the life of the times. Unfortunately many of the finest houses have disappeared. This undertaking to identify surviving homes, principally of the 17th and 18th centuries, has been inspired by a keen desire to honor and retain what is left of our historical heritage.

The outstanding chronicler of Norwich history was Frances Manwaring Caulkins, who published her first *History of Norwich* in 1845, which was followed in 1866 by a much larger and more complete revised edition. This contains a wealth of material and is the richest source available about the city's founding and development. This article is based largely on the 1866 edition. At the time of the Revolution Norwich was one of the twelve largest cities in the country. Many of its citizens, deeply concerned with the struggle for Independence, were important participants in many areas of that effort.

On June 6, 1659 Uncas sold for £70 the land which became Norwich. The deed was signed by Unkos, Owaneco and Attawanhood. That summer the activity was confined to surveying the town and laying out the home lots, clearing some land and making such other preliminary preparations as would enable the settlement to take place the following year. The town plot was laid out in a winding vale which followed the course of the circuitous Yantic River. A broad street or highway was opened through this valley, on each side of which the home lots were arranged. A pathway was likewise cleared from the center of the settlement to the first landing place below the falls of the Yantic near the head of the cove. This pathway corresponded in general to present Lafayette Street, to the point where it joins Yantic Street, which it followed down hill to the cove.

The land was in its natural wild state. It was a laborious task to cut down trees, to burn the underbrush, mark out lots and pathways, to throw temporary bridges over the runs of water, and to collect materials for building. The home lots each comprised a block of several acres and were in general river-lands favorable for mowing, pasture and tillage. Here lay a prime attraction to the new settlement, the first proprietors being, with scarcely a single exception, agriculturists and farmers. Each homestead had a tract of pasture land included in it or laid out as near to it as was convenient. Near the center of the town plot, an open space was left for public buildings and military parades. It was soon known as the Green or Plain.

Birds and animals of almost every species native to the climate were numerous to an uncommon degree. The Thames contained an abundance of fish — shad, alewives, bass, mackerel and eels. Oysters and lobsters were nowhere to be found in larger quantity or greater perfection. Just after the great freshet of February 1729, fish were so plentiful that 20,000 bass were caught within a few days just below the Landing. In 1771 it was reported that 300 barrels of mackerel were taken that season between Norwich and New London.

The settlers brought with them cattle and sheep, and at one time kept goats but the herds of these troublesome animals roamed at large until they became an intolerable nuisance. In 1660, wolves and foxes infested the area and the domestic animals were frequently attacked. Consequently the extermination of the wild animals was accomplished as rapidly as possible. The bounty for killing a wolf was 10s. 6d. but apparently was claimed only once after 1700, indicating that wolves were no longer troublesome. The bounty for rattlesnakes was originally 2d. per head but elimination of this hazard required a much longer time. In 1720 the bounty was doubled and was collected on 76 rattlesnakes. In 1721, 160 were slaughtered; by 1736 bounty was claimed on 112 snakes.

In settling a plantation one of the first necessities to be provided for was the grinding of corn. Maize was the common grain and a mill was indispensable. A town act of December 11, 1660 renews a contract with John Elderkin made in Saybrook for the erection of a grist mill. His first mill probably was erected in 1661 and was located in No Man's Acre (just above the Norwich falls) but this was soon removed to a situation below the falls. A first saw mill apparently was not set in operation until about 1700. Mr. Winthrop had a saw mill in New London and the first settlers in Norwich might have had some of their work done there, whence transportation by water was easy.

The appointment as an innkeeper was one of honor and respectability, and to obtain a license a man must have been of good report and possessed of a comfortable estate. The first of whom record remains was Simon Waterman, appointed December 11, 1679. About 1690 Deacon Simon Huntington received an appointment as innkeeper, and in 1701 Thomas Leffingwell was given liberty to "keep a publique house of entertainment for strangers." Taverns were used not only by travelers, but as a convenient meeting place where current events and private opinions might be circulated.

[2]

social

The history of the human race records that in all ages there have been far-sighted and clever people who endeavor to foresee the direction of future growth and benefit by acting in accordance with their judgment. While most of the settlers were agriculturists or artisans, the human desire to make profitable investments soon asserted itself. In addition to the excitement and romance of taking to the sea to trade with strange and distant lands, the speculative appeal of buying and selling vast tracts of land soon attracted the attention of those so inclined. Of course great gains are usually attended with great risks, but down through the ages there have been many willing to take those risks. The first large operator to appear on the Norwich scene was Major James Fitch (son of the Reverend James Fitch). By 1680 he had become well known for his extensive holdings. By legislative grants, by purchases from other grantees and intimate connection with the Indians, he accumulated a vast number of acres. He was a land surveyor, land registrar and land speculator who dealt on a great scale. As evidence of his activity in this area it is recorded that the town of Pomfret was founded on some 15,000 acres purchased from him. In the towns of Plainfield and Canterbury he owned land of such great extent as to be measured by miles.

At a later date the inventory of the estate of Christopher Leffingwell, who died in 1819, listed:

1 "right" in the Original Ohio purchase.

Land in the Connecticut Reserve in Ohio.

Land at Grafton, New Hampshire and Chittendon, Vt.

The trading of the early inhabitants must have been chiefly by barter. Clothing and provisions formed the circulating currency. No shopkeeper or merchant appears among the early inhabitants of Norwich. Alexander Pygan, an early merchant of New London, had 32 persons from Norwich with whom he had accounts before 1700. Boats frequently passed up and down the river and the beginning of commerce was soon beheld at the Landing Place.

As shipping grew, it was necessary to provide adequate landing and warehouse facilities. In 1684 a committee was appointed to lay out and bound for the town's use sufficient land for a public landing place and a suitable highway connected with it. In 1668 Major Fitch was allowed sufficient land near the waterside to accommodate a wharf and warehouse. In 1694 permission was given to establish a shipyard and in 1715-16 ships sailed for Barbados. In 1724 it was voted to build a town warehouse at the Landing Place. In 1734 permission was given to Lieut. Simon Lathrop to build a warehouse.

A brief interruption is made here to indicate the economic progress of the early settlers. The inventory of the estate of Ensign Thomas Leffingwell, who died on March 5, 1724 in his 75th year, totalled £9,793, 9s. and 11d. Apparently he did not rely alone on land speculation, but accumulated his estate through his ability, good judgment and diligence. There is no record of any other estate in the town that equalled this in value at that time. This is a striking example of the rewards available to those hardworking and thrifty pioneers.

Over 150 years later, in 1888, the Norwich Board of Trade issued a booklet to attract new industry. In the statistical section the manufacturing concerns then

[3]

operating are listed, showing among other things the number of employees and the annual payroll. Herewith is the report for the largest companies:

Textiles	Hands	Annual Payroll	Average Earnings per Employee
Ponemah Mills	1500	$ 450,000	$300
Falls Company	550	160,000	291
Shetucket Company	500	150,000	300
Norwich Bleaching, Dyeing & Printing	350	200,000	571
Totoket Mill	250	50,000	200
Yantic Woolen	150	50,000	333
	3300		
Other			
Chelsea Paper Mfg.	230	120,000	522
Hopkins & Allen Fire Arms Co.	175	120,000	686
Norwich & Worcester Car & Machine Shop	175	120,000	686
Richmond Stove	150	100,000	666
	4030	$1,520,000	$377

It will be noted that the textile industry was the largest employer and that their annual employee wage was roughly one-half that of other manufacturers. The fact that the overall annual average was only $377.00—one hundred and sixty-three years after Thomas Leffingwell's death—brings into sharp relief the amazing value of his estate if translated into the present value of the dollar.

To return to the development of commerce, probably before 1730 four sloops owned in Norwich were engaged in the West India and the coasting trade. In 1732 the Norwich "scooner, Nath: Shaw master," came in from Ireland. At about that time vessels were frequently built in the river at Norwich where timber was plentiful, and some were sent elsewhere to be sold. One of these shipbuilders was Joseph Kelley who had been given permission to build vessels at the Landing Place. In 1751 he was notified that in 12 months he would have to cease building his vessels there, "the place being much wanted for public employment," being required for loading and unloading of ships. The interest in navigation continued to increase steadily. In the *New London Summary*, the first newspaper issued in this part of the colony, which began in 1758, advertisements of Norwich vessels were frequently inserted.

The Norwich importers usually owned their own vessels. Many articles of commerce might easily have been manufactured at home but Parliamentary restraints prevented this. Such items as felt hats, nails, paper, loaf sugar, snuff and spices were imported. Also ribbons, crepes, laces, printed linens, chintzes, and damasks, plain linens and Holland cotton in the piece were among the items frequently imported. The dry goods and fancy articles were in best assortment uptown at the shops near the Norwichtown Green and the ladies were accustomed to go there to do their shopping.

Typical of the mercantile establishments (circa 1765) was that of John Baker Bremmer "who keeps a little of everything and gives cash for ox horns, old pewter and hopps." Isaiah Tiffany keeps "ribbons, fans, calicos, lawns and chinaware just imported from London." At that time the invoice value of shipments from Great Britain ranged from a few hundred to three or four thousand pounds annually. The stock was often oddly assorted. For instance, one man advertised sheep's wool, cod fish, West India products and European dry goods and "he expects to have New England rum constantly to sell." Included in the dress goods offered for sale were satins, broadcloth, hum-hum, wild-bore, elasticks, moreens, durants, calimancos, tammys, royal-rib, shalloons, erminetts, stockinetts, russeletts, German serge, duffles, taffety.

Other business activities were developing also. Dr. Daniel Lathrop, who graduated from Yale in 1733, furthered his medical studies in London. He returned to Norwich and established the only apothecary shop on the route from New York to Boston. Benedict Arnold was one of his apprentices and later established an apothecary shop in New Haven.

In 1750 an iron works was established in the parish of New Concord (Bozrah). Elijah Backus commenced a similar works at Yantic at approximately the same time. He manufactured blooming and bar iron for anchors, mills and other uses. The Backus Iron Works earned great repute and during the Revolutionary War all kinds of iron work necessary for domestic use and various instruments of warfare were made and repaired at the Yantic forge. In 1766 cutlery made its appearance as a business and various implements of husbandry that before had been imported were manufactured in town. Ebenezer Colburn was an ironmonger and cutler.

The first postal service in this area was a regular stage route to Providence. Individuals were engaged to ride weekly to all the major cities in the vicinity, conveying letters, papers and small bundles. In 1774 regular weekly communication was established between Norwich and Boston for which £60 per annum was subscribed. The post left Norwich every Thursday, reached Boston on Saturday, and started back to Norwich the following Monday. The New London office was the station for letter delivery for all the eastern border of Connecticut to Woodstock and Pomfret to the north, and from Guilford to Westerly on Long Island sound.

The first Norwich post office established by the Federal Government was located next door to the Meeting House in 1782. The first postmaster, Dudley Woodbridge, served for eight years and was succeeded by William and Christopher Leffingwell who kept office on Leffingwell corner. At this time the mails went twice a week by three stage routes, Hartford via Windham, New Haven via New London, and Boston via Providence. In 1803 a post office was established at the Landing and was entitled "Chelsea Landing." In 1827 that post office name was changed to Norwich City. In 1836 that post office was changed to Norwich, and the one on the Norwichtown Green was changed to Norwichtown.

The various acts of Parliament aroused resentment in opposition. The Stamp Act was passed in March 1764 to take effect November 1st. Thomas Fitch, who was Governor of Connecticut at that time, decided to support it. In meeting with his Council to advise them of that fact, seven of the eleven present remonstrated

[5]

vigorously and then withdrew indignantly. This incident gives a good indication of the temper of the times. It became obvious that the Colonies should become independent not only in the field of government but economically as well. A list of articles was promulgated which would not be imported, purchased or used if produced or manufactured outside of North America. In this list of over 30 categories were cordage and anchors, sole leather, deck nails, clocks, wrought plate, shoes. These items could be produced here.

In 1766 a pottery was established at Bean Hill. That same year Christopher Leffingwell established his paper mill on the Yantic River (just above the Canada Bridges). This was the first paper mill in Connecticut. A merchants' committee in 1770 recommended to the wealthy persons in town to enter into subscriptions for setting up and carrying on the making of nails, stocking-weaving and other useful branches of manufacture, and every one in his respective sphere of action was encouraged to promote industry and frugality. There was an immediate response to this clarion call. The determination to become economically self-sufficient and independent of England as rapidly as possible resulted in the establishment of many new enterprises and this period marks the beginning of Norwich as an important manufacturing center. In 1770 Christopher Leffingwell established a fulling mill with dye house attached, and a chocolate mill which was operated by water power. In 1772 a fulling mill was established by Simon Huntington, chocolate mills were put in operation, pot and pearl ashes (potash) were made by the calcination of hardwoods.

The manufacture of cut shingle-nails from old iron hoops was started by Edmund Darrow. This was one of the first attempts in this country to make nails in a way less slow and tedious than the old operation of hammering them out of solid iron. Between 1773 and 1780 four fulling-mills with clothier's shops and dye-houses went into operation. In 1773 Thomas Harland commenced the business of clock and watch-making and silversmithing. He taught a number of apprentices. In 1778 he superintended the construction of the first fire engine owned in Norwich. That same year Noah Hidden established a comb-making business and at about the same time Alvan Fosdick undertook the manufacture of cards. Other artisans who established themselves in business at about this time were a gunsmith from Preston, England, a tape-weaver from Manchester, and Richard Collier, a brazier.

The first newspaper to be published in Norwich was the *Norwich Packet,* started in 1773. This was produced by Robertsons and Trumbull. That same year the printing press of Green & Spooner was set up where they published pamphlets and books. In 1774 Nathaniel Patten, a bookbinder and stationer, "offered for sale the largest assortment of books that had probably ever been displayed in this part of Connecticut." Samuel Loudon opened a shop at the Landing with a large assortment of books.

In 1775 William Lax established a manufactory of gun carriages in town, and succeeded so well as to be employed by the State to furnish apparatus for much of the cannon used by them. The Elijah Backus forge on the Yantic was busily engaged in the manufacture of ship anchors—two of which weighed 1200 lbs.

each—for the State's armed vessels. He afterwards engaged in casting cannon. Samuel Noyes made and repaired guns and bayonets for the light-infantry.

The blockade of the coast by British war vessels soon created scarcities in various essential products. In 1775 shortages of salt and wheat developed which required rationing and careful distribution.

After recovering from the first blow of the Revolution the inhabitants of Norwich were not only alert in turning their attention to various industrial pursuits, but were engaged also in the brilliant chance game of privateering. The War therefore, while it exhausted the strength and resources of neighboring towns that lay exposed upon the sea-coast, acted as a spur to the enterprise of Norwich. The town was admirably situated to serve as a port of refuge to which vessels could retire and discharge their cargoes in safety.

New London, at the mouth of the river, was depressed in all her interests, kept in continual alarm, and finally by the blazing torch of the enemy almost swept from the face of the earth. But Norwich, securely seated at the head of the river, defended by her hills and nourished by her valleys, planting and reaping without fear of invasion or loss, not only built new shops and dwelling houses, and engaged with spirit and success in a variety of new manufactures, but entered vigorously into ship-building and boldly sent out her vessels to bring in spoils from the ocean.

After 1780 the farms too prospered, the mechanical arts flourished, and there was almost a superabundance, not merely in the means of living, but of articles of luxury and display. In 1781 and 1782 the town was overflowing with merchandise, both tropical and European. The goods were mostly obtained by successful privateering.

The end of the Revolution in 1783 was followed by a great revival of maritime activity. The West Indies trade offered an alluring path of adventure and profit. Horses, catttle and farm produce of a thriving back country converged at Norwich and sought a market abroad. It was prosecuted with vigor, and was rich in its returns. Livestock, provisions and lumber were the articles demanded for the West Indies market. Considerable wheat was raised in eastern Connecticut and flour was then an article of export from this area. The Norwich vessels seldom took in their livestock from the wharves. Sheep and swine might be received directly from the land here, but horses, oxen and cows were driven to New London and there taken on board. It was rare for a vessel to carry her deck cargo down the river. The goods imported in return, in order of greatest value, consisted of sugar, molasses, European goods, rum, coffee and hides.

The quantity of livestock carried even by the smaller vessels or sloops was astonishing. For instance, in 1789 the *Betsey* took out 35 horses and the *Nancy*, 36. These were small sloops. The brig *Neptune* carried 49 horses and the *Enterpriser*, besides provisions, brick and lumber, carried 20 horses, 17 cattle, nine mules, 20 sheep, 20 swine, 150 geese and 100 turkeys. In 1798 Capt. Isaac Hull, in the employ of Norwich and New London merchants, sailed from New London with 98 oxen on his deck.

The repeated shipments of livestock to the West Indies which were put aboard at New London after having been driven overland from Norwich to New London, created a demand for a turnpike, and in 1791 a lottery was drawn to make the Norwich-New London road into a turnpike and to erect a toll gate. Toll commenced in June, 1792—a 4-wheeled carriage paid 9d., a 2-wheeled carriage 4½d., a man and horse 1d. Miss Caulkins says that this was the first turnpike in the United States but it is now believed to have been the first in New England and the second in the United States. It became an important thoroughfare and a great service to Norwich and the towns to her rear in transporting produce to New London for embarkation. The original turnpike started in Norwich at the Norwichtown Green. In 1806 a connection was made from the warehouse bridge in Chelsea South to join the turnpike at Trading Cove. The Norwich to Providence post road was made a turnpike in 1794 and the Norwich and Woodstock road was made a turnpike in 1801.

The rushing tide of traffic set with steady current toward the tropics. Trade with Europe was re-established but with diminished enterprise. At times a fishing voyage was combined with European trade. A license for fishing and a foreign passport were obtained, the vessel cleared for the cod fisheries and then proceeded to market their catch abroad, using the funds thus acquired to purchase a cargo to bring back to Norwich. The first collector of U. S. customs under the Federal Constitution was General Jedidiah Huntington of Norwich, appointed by General Washington. General Huntington immediately relinquished his mercantile concerns, removed to New London, and took possession of his office August 11, 1789 at 7:00 a.m.

In the period 1790 to 1800 the Norwichtown Green was the location of four or five stores, three taverns, two printing offices with book shop and bindery attached, retail stores and work shops dotted the whole way from Bean Hill to Chelsea. In 1790 Dr. Joshua Lathrop commenced cotton manufacture with six jennies, six looms, and a carding machine. In 1794 Jay's treaty with England temporarily ended British interference with United States shipping and American commerce resumed its flourishing course. In 1795 a list of the ships and their tonnage whose home port was Norwich totaled 42 vessels with combined tonnage of 4312 tons. This does not include a number of river packets to and from New York.

The activity in shipping, manufacturing and trade resulted in the accumulation of much wealth and there were many families who were able to satisfy their desires for the finer things of life. Houghton Bulkeley wrote in *Craftsmen & Artists of Norwich:* "Norwich homes and their furnishings kept pace with its economic prosperity. The furniture made or owned in Norwich did not lag behind the economy, and many of the outstanding examples of Connecticut craftsmanship can be traced to the Norwich area." Mr. Bulkeley lists 66 Norwich cabinet makers. Similarly there were 49 silversmiths, and 20 clockmakers, 12 of whom were also silversmiths and are included in the total of 49 of the latter.

The increasing cost and value of the homes of this prosperous period logically suggested the desirability of establishing insurance companies. In 1794 the Norwich Mutual Assurance Co. was granted a charter. The first meeting was held at the old Courthouse in Norwich, December 28, 1794. The Norwich Marine Insurance Co. was chartered in 1803. The Fire Insurance Co. was organized in 1813. The New London County Mutual Fire Insurance was chartered in May, 1840.

Industrial development continued. In 1803 a hemp mill was started but did not operate for long, the factory being purchased and changed to a cotton mill in 1813. This was one of the first cotton mills to operate in this country. Howland, Brown & Co., circa 1800, owned and fitted out the ship *Charlotte,* and some 15 or 20 brigs, schooners and sloops; often they had on hand livestock sufficient for two or three deck-loads to the West Indies. A foundry at the west end of the warehouse bridge was operating in 1805. Goddard & Williams were flour merchants and manufacturers at the Falls. Williams later entered the whaling business.

War was declared by the United States on June 19, 1812. New London was blockaded by British ships, commerce on the Thames ceased at once. A few privateers eluded the blockade but others were captured. Because imports were stopped, war gave a decided impetus to manufacture. Between 1813 and 1816 four cotton mills were established, two woolen mills and a nail factory. Tidings of the war's end reached Norwich February 13, 1815 and was greeted with enthusiasm. The War of 1812 depressed business in Norwich to a considerable extent and terminated the palmy days of West Indian trade.

In 1813 a nail factory was established at the Falls. Nails were cut by a newly invented machine which was a great improvement over former methods. In 1823 Falls water power was utilized to run the Thames Manufacturing Co. which was the forerunner of the Falls Mill. In 1826 Quinebaug Co. was chartered to manufacture cotton and woolen goods. This was the first mill in Greenville. In 1837 there was a financial crash which created a period of depression and stagnation of business. The Quinebaug Co. was sold to become the Shetucket Mills (now Atlantic Carton Corp.), and the Thames Manufacturing Co. was sold to become the Falls Mill.

In 1818 Amos H. Hubbard had started a paper mill at the Falls and in 1860 this mill was sold to the Falls Co. and the Hubbard Paper Co. was established in Greenville. In 1828 a woolen mill was established at Bean Hill and another mill soon after by Peter Lanman. That same year the Norwich Water Power Co. was incorporated to develop the Greenville water privilege. From the dam a canal was dug 45 feet wide, 9 feet deep and $\frac{7}{8}$ of a mile long. Along this canal factories for the manufacture of cotton goods, paper, flannel and carpets sprang up.

On October 15, 1816 Capt. Bunker in the steamboat *Connecticut* ascended the Thames to Norwich. "People from the neighborhood rushed to the place to behold the prodigy that science had produced," wrote Miss Caulkins. A regular line of steam communication with New York started in 1817. The *Connecticut* and the *Fulton* were the ships of the line. The (sailing) packet system from that time on lost its patronage and importance. The merchants of Norwich and New London were mutually interested in communication with New York by a line of steamboats. The Norwich and New London Steamboat Co. was organized in 1848 with a capital of $200,000. They ran their boats in connection with the Norwich and Worcester Railroad terminating at Allyn's Point. This company was dissolved in 1860 but in that same year the Norwich and New York Transportation Co. was organized with a capital of $350,000. This was formed for the purpose of facilitating the operations of the Norwich and Worcester Railroad by furnishing an advantageous connection with New York. In 1862 the gross earnings for 16 months was $466,227 and the growth of this business is indicated by the fact that in 1865 the gross business for 12 months was $704,198.

The rapid growth of the financial resources of the business organizations and amazing accumulation of capital is attested by the following chronology of the formation of commercial banks:

	Total Capital
The Norwich Bank incorporated 1796, $150,000 capital.	
1864 changed to the Norwich National Bank	$ 150,000
1825 the Thames Bank organized capital $200,000 and in 1856 this was increased to $500,000, and in 1865 to $1,000,000; now the Thames Branch of the Connecticut Bank & Trust Co.	1,000,000
1832 the Quinebaug Bank organized, capital $500,000. In 1864 became the First National Bank of Norwich	500,000
1833 the Merchants Bank organized, capital $200,000	200,000
1856 the Shetucket Bank organized with $100,000 and became the Shetucket National Bank in 1864	100,000
1855 the Uncas Bank organized, $300,000 capital	300,000
This combined with the Merchants Bank in 1928, forming the Uncas-National Bank became branch 1955 of the Hartford National Bank.	
1864 the Second National Bank organized, capital $100,000, later increased to $300,000	300,000
	$2,550,000

The Savings Banks were established as follows:

Norwich Savings Society in 1824
Chelsea Savings Bank   in 1858
Dime Savings Bank   in 1869

This was the period when many of the handsome Greek Revival houses on Washington Street and Broadway were constructed, several of which have disappeared from the scene in recent years.

The Norwich and Worcester Railroad Co. was formed in 1832. Construction was started in 1835 and completed so that trains ran over the whole distance in 1840. The distance from Norwich to Worcester by rail was 58.9 miles. Following a spring flood in 1841 a sandbar formed below the Norwich harbor which interfered with shipping to Norwich. In 1843 the railroad was extended south to Allyn's Point.

In 1847 the State of Connecticut granted a charter to the New London, Willimantic & Springfield Co. to build a railroad. In 1848 application was made for an Act of the Legislature to unite this company with the New London, Willimantic and Palmer R.R. Co. In 1849 the stockholders of both companies voted to merge under the name of the New London, Willimantic and Palmer Railroad Co. This railroad later became known as the New

London Northern (Central Vermont) Railroad. Regular operations began in September, 1850. Three years later that company voted to accept the proposal of the Norwich & Worcester Railroad for a connection between the two railroads at Norwich.

There is record of the fact that in May 1847 it was proposed in New London that a bridge be built across the Thames at that point. The Town Record of Norwich records that it was "voted to oppose with the utmost vigor the petition of New London to bridge the Thames, as such a measure would be very injurious to the interests of this town." The sum of $5000 was appropriated to carry out this vote.

In 1882 permission was given by the General Assembly to construct a bridge across the Thames River between New London and Groton. Actual construction began in 1888 and was concluded in 1889. The bridge accommodated a double track railroad and comprised the necessary link to permit direct rail connection from New York to Boston via the shore line. The bridge presented an engineering problem on account of the width of the channel, which was solved by a swing draw 503 feet in length.

In 1853 the Norwich Gas Light Co. was formed. Shortly thereafter the Norwich City Gas Co. was formed in competition. The two companies consolidated in 1858. On July 1, 1904 the City purchased the properties of the Norwich Gas & Electric Company, and since that time they have been operated as a municipal plant.

The Cold Spring Iron Works was established in Thamesville by Thomas Mitchell in 1845. He originally came from England to Wareham, Mass., then to Norwich to take charge of this concern. This same year a rolling mill was built. In 1855 vessels were built nearly under the Shetucket River bridge but this shipyard was transferred to Thamesville near the Iron Works soon thereafter. The rolling mill and shipyard were the beginning of the prosperous village of Thamesville. In 1863 the Thames Iron Works built another rolling mill in this vicinity. In 1860 a cork factory was established at the Falls. The Civil War developed an astonishing activity in armories and machine shops. Sail makers' lofts were engaged in making tents.

This record has been compiled to give a brief outline of the economic importance and substance of Norwich during its earlier years. No attempt has been made to bring the record up to the present day.

At the time of the Revolution, Norwich was the home of Samuel Huntington, Signer of the Declaration of Independence and President of the Continental Congress from September 1779 to July 1781. Before the adoption of the Constitution in 1787, the Continental Congress was the supreme governing body in the country and its President was the equivalent of the President of the United States today. The Huntington family in Norwich also furnished three Generals: General Jabez Huntington, General Jedidiah Huntington, who later was appointed by General Washington to be the first Collector of Customs, and General Ebenezer Huntington. Christopher Leffingwell was one of the organizers and financial supporters of the expedition to capture Fort Ticonderoga with its huge store of military supplies, accomplished by

Ethan Allen and his Green Mountain boys. The patriotic ardor burned brightly in Norwich and the entire community supported the War of Independence with great fervor.

Mrs. Ada R. Chase, active in The Society of Founders for many years and Norwich's greatly respected historian, wrote a paper about illustrious sons of Norwich which adds much to the picture of Old Norwich. Just before her death in November, 1966 she graciously permitted the following condensation from her paper.

There were six Presidents of the United States with Norwich ancestry— Millard Fillmore, Ulysses S. Grant, Rutherford B. Hayes, James A. Garfield, Grover Cleveland and Franklin Delano Roosevelt. Millard Fillmore, the thirteenth President, took office in 1850. He was the great, great grandson of John Fillmore of Ipswich, Massachusetts. His son, Captain John, married Mary Spiller and came to Norwich West Farms (Franklin) where he died February 22, 1777. His great, great grandson, Millard Fillmore was born January 7, 1800 in Summer Hill, New York. President Fillmore cherished his connection with Norwich and was its honored guest at the Bi-Centennial Celebration in 1859.

Christopher Huntington, the first male child born in Norwich (November 1, 1660) was the ancestor of Ulysses S. Grant, our eighteenth President. His granddaughter, Martha Huntington, married Noah Grant of Tolland on June 12, 1717. Their son Noah, Jr., married Susannah Delano and their son, Noah III, married Rachel Kelley. They had a son Jesse, born January 23, 1794, married Hannah Simpson June 24, 1821, and their son Ulysses S. Grant was born April 27, 1822 and became President in 1869.

George Hayes left Scotland in 1680 and settled in Windsor, Connecticut, in 1682. His great, great, great grandson, Rutherford Hayes, settled at Brattleboro, Vermont, and in September 1813 married Sophio Birchard. Her ancestry on the male side is traced to John Birchard, one of the thirty-five founders of Norwich. Rutherford died in Delaware, Ohio, in 1822, three months before the birth of his son Rutherford Birchard Hayes, who became the nineteenth President in 1877.

James A. Garfield took office in 1881 as the twentieth President. He came from a long line of New England forefathers, which included Major John Mason and the Reverend James Fitch, the leaders of the sturdy little band who settled Norwich in 1659-60.

Grover Cleveland became the twenty-second President in 1885. He was descended from William Hyde, a founder. The Reverend Aaron Cleveland married Abiah Hyde. With great versatility he not only prepared his sermons, but also wrote poems, essays and carried on a hat making industry. He was the great grandfather of the President. His son, William, carried on the business of a gold and silversmith until his death in 1837. Cleveland silver is highly prized by collectors .

The second Mrs. Theodore Roosevelt was Edith Kermit Carew, born in Norwich August 6, 1862. Her grandfather was General Daniel Tyler of Brooklyn, Connecticut, and Norwich. Mrs. Roosevelt bought the old Tyler house in Brooklyn and for many years spent part of each summer there.

At least seventeen ancestors of President Franklin Delano Roosevelt lie buried in the Norwichtown cemetery. The roots of his ancestry go back through many channels to the founders, identifying with the Huntington, Adgate, Gager, Bill, Howland, Perkins, Lathrop and Clark families. On July 1, 1934, the Society of the Founders of Norwich erected a tablet over the grave of Captain Ephraim Bill (died Nov. 14, 1802) and Lydia Huntington Bill, his wife (died Sept. 23, 1798) in the Oak Street Cemetery, Norwich. They were the great, great, great grandparents of President Roosevelt.

Governors of Connecticut with Norwich roots were:

Samuel Huntington	1786-96
Roger Sherman Baldwin	1844-46
William Alfred Buckingham, LLD.	1858-66
Simeon E. Baldwin, LLD.	1911-15
Hiram Bingham	1925
Wilbur Lewis Cross	1931-39

* * *

This preface is intended to establish a frame of reference from which the houses illustrated and described in this volume may be better understood and appreciated. It is regrettable that the "march of time" has destroyed several of the distinguished homes that embellished this scene. That fact, and the earnest desire to preserve as much of the remaining ancestral heritage as possible, has led to the movement to establish an Historic District in the Norwichtown area, under the provisions of Public Act No. 430 enacted by the 1961 General Assembly of the State of Connecticut. Few towns in the State, and even in all New England, have a heritage of which they can be so proud.

[13]

Key to the Letters Used in the House Descriptions

A — Original or early owner.

B — Date built.

C — Position of house.

D — Type of construction.

E — Roof.

F — Chimney.

G — Height.

H — Ell.

I — Windows.

J — Foundation.

K — Interesting features.

* * *

THE NORWICHTOWN GREEN

On April 28, 1729, the Town Proprietors voted that the Meetinghouse Plain "shall be and remain to be . . . for publick Use for the whole Town forever hereafter without Alteration."

The Meetinghouse Plain, now known as the Norwichtown Green, was the site of the first settlement in Norwich in 1659. The first Meetinghouse was built here in 1660. Later the plain was used as a training ground for Revolutionary troops.

At the southern end stood the old Court House, where the Mutual Assurance Company of the City of Norwich, the first insurance company incorporated in the State, was established in 1795.

81 *EAST TOWN STREET*
FIRST CONGREGATIONAL CHURCH OF NORWICHTOWN

This Church is the fifth meeting house erected in Norwich.

The first meeting house, built about 1660, stood near the southeast corner of the Green. The second meeting house, erected in 1675, was on the summit of Meeting House Rocks and served as a lookout against Indian raids during King Philip's War. The third meeting house was built on the hill near the site of the old one and completed in 1713.

The fourth Church was built at the corner of the Green, completed in 1770 and consumed to ashes in 1801 by a fire of incendiary origin. The cornerstone of the present Church, the fifth, was laid on June 18, 1801, by General Ebenezer Huntington.

The existing building is representative of the period when the huge, barnlike structures of the 18th century were becoming more ornate. This is evidenced by the square two-story tower and projecting portico which repeats the rather flat lines of the roof and the corner quoins of the main building. The structure was extensively remodeled in 1845 and in later years.

A—First Congregational Church
B—1801
C—Faces east
D—Wood
E—Peak, very flat
F—1 brick, end
G—Two stories and a half
I—Arched. Double tier on each side of second floor
J—Stone
K—A square, two-story tower rises at front with a projecting portico. The corner quoins are the same as those on the main building. Two round topped and one square headed windows on the second floor provide an unusual fenestration, the principle ornament sky blue.

MEETING-HOUSE ROCKS

IN 1673 ON THE SUMMIT OF
THESE ROCKS WAS ERECTED THE
SECOND MEETING HOUSE BUILT
IN THE TOWN OF NORWICH, WHICH
SERVED ALSO AS A WATCH TOWER
AGAINST THE INDIANS ....

EAST TOWN STREET
MEETING HOUSE ROCKS

The rocky ledge west of the Norwichtown
Congregational Church was the site in 1675
of the second meeting house in Norwich.
The place served a three-fold purpose as a
place of worship, as a watchtower against
the Indians and as a garrison post. It is now
a site for outdoor worship by the First Congregational Church.

[16]

77 *EAST TOWN STREET*
JESSE BROWN TAVERN

Close-up of Iron Fence

Jesse Brown married Anna Rudd, daughter of Nathaniel and Mary (Backus) Rudd of Franklin, Connecticut in 1769. They had six children. He participated in the Revolution by officiating as the Governor's Post. As express agent and confidential messenger, he relayed the news of the occupation of Philadelphia by the British under Lord Howe. In 1781 he married his wife's cousin, Lucy Rudd, daughter of Daniel and Mary (Metcalf) Rudd.

In 1790 he was licensed to open a tavern. He became the stage contractor and established lines between Boston and New York via Providence and Norwich.

A—Jesse Brown
B—1787-90
C—Faces East
D—Wood
E—Peak
F—1 brick end and 1 brick central
G—Two stories and a half
H—Long 2-story ell on outer ends, East and West
I—9 windows front, 6/6 sash, French type windows on first story extend to porch floor
J—Stone
K—Extensively altered

On Wednesday evening, August 1, 1797 President John Adams and his wife were guests at the Jesse Brown Tavern. He was welcomed by the Matross Company in full uniform and honored with a sixteen-gun salute.

One of his daughters, Ann, married John Vernet who built the lovely home located at 118 Washington Street. The famous Vernet grape was first cultivated in the garden of Jesse Brown's Tavern. Mr. Brown died in 1818 in Wilkes Barre, Pennsylvania, where he lived with the Vernet family.

Extensively altered, it has been known as the Rock Nook Home for Children. The United Workers, the present owner, constitute the organized charities of Norwich and serve as The Public Health Agency.

73 *EAST TOWN STREET*
SILVERSMITH SHOP

Joseph Carpenter was born in 1747, son of Joseph and Elizabeth (Lathrop) Carpenter. In 1775 he married Eunice, daughter of Ebenezer and Mary (Huntington) Fitch. They had a family of six children and their last known residence was in the Chelsea Parade area.

He had this shop built for him between 1772 and 1774. He was one of the most successful of the Norwich silversmiths, clockmakers and pewterers and his products are collectors' items. He made jewelry, clocks and engravings. He shared the shop with his brother, Gardner, who operated a mercantile business.

The shop stayed in the Carpenter family until 1915 and was restored by Norman Morrison Isham, Architect, in 1916. It is believed that this is the only silversmith shop to survive in New England. The Society of the Founders of Norwich, Connecticut, Inc., acquired the building in 1956.

A—Joseph Carpenter
B—1772-1773
C—East
D—Wood
E—Gambrel
F—1-end, brick
G—Story and a half
I—Outside wooden fold-up shutters
J—Fieldstone
K—Restored

69 EAST TOWN STREET
DR. DANIEL LATHROP SCHOOL

This small building with its wooden belfry is one of the earliest brick school houses still standing in the State. The school was named for Dr. Daniel Lathrop because of his efforts in fostering its erection. Dr. Lathrop left a legacy of £500 for an endowed free grammar school in 1782. Later it was occupied by the Noah Webster Literary Association. It is now used by the City of Norwich for municipal elections.

A—Town of Norwich
B—1783
C—Faces East
D—Brick with wooden belfry
E—Gambrel
F—1 brick, end
G—Story and a half
I—4 windows and door; 12/12 sash
J—Squared stone

12 MEDITERRANEAN LANE
CAPTAIN RICHARD CHARLTON HOUSE

This charming hideaway was built as a retreat between voyages by Captain Charlton prior to 1757. He was killed in the capture of Havana in that year. He was born in England and it is believed that he was a Huguenot. He married Sarah, daughter of Thomas and Ann (Birchard) Grist. They had six children and when he died, his widow inherited the building. At her death their son Charles inherited the homestead. He left Norwich soon after this and his brother Samuel became the owner. It is believed Samuel altered the building to its present design.

The building has 17th century framing with a summer beam seventeen inches across and gun stock corner posts. Many feel Charlton may have used the frame of an older building when he constructed this cabin. The doorway is flanked by bull's-eye glass. The house nestles against a cliff and its furnishings and setting denote the peace and charm of its years.

A—Richard Charlton
B—Prior to 1757 (Source: Perkins and Owner)
C—Faces East
D—Wood
E—Peak
F—1 brick, central
G—Story and half
I—3 windows each side of front door; 6/6 sash
J—Stone
K—Completely restored. Interior: Three rooms downstairs with a loft above. Very narrow steps to loft. Living room floor slants slightly toward the door to facilitate floor washing for the sea captain. Exterior: Main door on East side with bull's-eye glass. Another entrance on South side.

55 EAST TOWN STREET
GARDNER CARPENTER HOUSE

Gardner Carpenter was born in 1749, son of Joseph and Elizabeth (Lathrop) Carpenter. In 1791 he married Mary, daughter of Benjamin and Mary (Carew) Brown and they had six children. In 1793 he bought this property from Benjamin Butler with a house on the lot. He then removed the original home and built his house.

He was one of the better known retail business men of the era. He maintained a mercantile business in half of the shop that he shared with his brother, Joseph Carpenter, the silversmith.

During the Revolutionary War he served as a paymaster in the Seventeenth Connecticut Regiment in 1776. He was appointed as postmaster in Norwich in January, 1799 and held this office for fifteen years. He died in 1815 and Mary died in 1838. This house is often referred to as the Red House.

A—Gardner Carpenter
B—1793-94
C—Faces East
D—Brick
E—Peak originally, gambrel at present due to third story addition by Joseph Huntington in 1816.
F—Two, end, brick, one also on rear wall of main house and one modern chimney in the rear wing.
G—2½ stories
H—Several one-story additions at the rear of the house. In 1958 a one story addition in the rear family-room. Other additions removed during this process.
I—9 windows front; 6/6 sash. Brick lintels on first story.
J—Rough coursed ashlar
K—Overhang at 2nd story end. Small gabled porch built over front door is supported by round columns. Interior is original, with old paneling.

[21]

2 ELM AVENUE
SIMON HUNTINGTON, JR., TAVERN

Simon Huntington was born in 1659 in Saybrook, the son of Deacon Simon and Sarah (Clark) Huntington. In 1683 he married Lydia, daughter of John Gager of Norwich. The couple had four children.

Simon Huntington, Jr., was very active in the early community in civic matters, as land holder, and in the office of Deacon of the Church. In 1694 he was given liberty to keep "A house of public entertainment." Innkeepers in those days were considered town officers. The appointment was one of honor and respectability. He succeeded Sgt. Thomas Waterman in title.

The center portion of his home was used as a munitions magazine for the defensive weapons of the town as late as 1720. He died in 1736 and willed some of his properties to his son and the house to his widow.

In 1768 Ebenezer, his son, willed the house to his son, Simon, who sold it to Thomas Carey. Carey then sold it to Joseph Carew, who remodeled and enlarged the old house, using parts of it to rebuild it as we see it today.

A—Simon Huntington, Jr.
B—1690
C—Faces West
D—Wood
E—Peak
F—2 new brick at ends
G—Two stories and a half
I—9-window front with ell containing 2 windows to South, 12/12 sash.

8 ELM AVENUE
SARAH KNIGHT TAVERN

The André Richards home was built in 1734, probably by adding to or enlarging the original dwelling of Sarah Knight. Little is known of André Richards but there is a sketchy, interesting record of Sarah Knight.

Sarah Knight was born in 1665 in Boston. She first appeared in Norwich in 1698. Her status was Storekeeper, Innkeeper and widow. After a few years in Norwich she returned to Boston.

In 1704 she made her famous horseback journey from Boston to New York, keeping a diary that gives a graphic description of provincial New England.

She reappeared in Norwich in 1717 and that year gave to the Church a silver communion cup. The town voted her permission to resume using the pew she had previously occupied. The communion cup is now on display in the Boston Museum of Fine Arts.

Another active Innkeeper to reside here was Joseph Peck. He bought the house of Capt. Philip Turner about 1754, and possibly enlarged it. The house was then known as Peck's Tavern and was very popular prior to the Revolutionary War.

A—André Richard
B—1698-1734
C—Faces West
D—Wood
E—Peak
F—Stone and brick, 2 central
G—Two stories and a half
I—4 windows North of front door, 8 windows South; 6/6 sash
J—Stone
K—Exterior: Front yard enclosed with old iron fence; very large elm in front. Interior: South end of house is in original building. The large kitchen with enclosed fireplace may be of the Sarah Knight building.

14 ELM AVENUE
LATHROP HOUSE

In 1747 William Morgan of Groton, Connecticut, came into possession of this property and this house was built between 1747 and 1752. In 1757 the house was sold to Nathan Stedman, a prominent attorney. He, Dr. Daniel Lathrop and Capt. Philip Turner were responsible for laying out Water Street in the downtown Norwich area. Stedman sold the house to Azariah Lathrop in 1764 who enlarged it. The Lathrop family then owned the property for several years.

Dr. Gurdon Lathrop, Azariah's son, lived here. He was either a druggist or a medical doctor by the title, but we assume he was a druggist because he operated a shop across the Green in 1791. Gerard Lathrop, fourth son of Azariah, inherited the house in 1810. There have been several owners since.

A—William Morgan
B—1747-1752
C—Faces West
D—Wood
E—Hip monitor
F—2 brick, central
G—Two stories and a half
H—2 story on Northeast end
I—4 windows on each side of front door, 1 window above door; 6/6 sash; windows have "bricked" moulding above the key in center.
J—Stone
K—Heavy brackets under roof line on all four sides. Small square "lookout" with windows on four sides built in center of roof between the two chimneys; has small low railing around the outside. Slight gable to front of house in two stories—no break in roof line.

85 *TOWN STREET*
DIAH MANNING HOUSE

Samuel Manning, born in 1723, married Anne Winship in 1746. He died in 1783 and his widow, Anne, daughter Eunice and son Diah inherited the house.

Diah was born in 1760. In 1784 he married Anna Gifford, daughter of James and Susanna (Hubbard) Gifford. He and his brother, Roger, served as drummers in the Revolutionary War. In 1775 Roger was in Colonel Israel Putnam's regiment and Diah in the 8th Regiment under Colonel Jedediah Huntington. At Valley Forge in 1778 both brothers were chosen to be in Washington's Body Guard, Diah being designated Drum Major. Diah carried to Major André his last breakfast on the morning of his execution.

Diah's family was extremely kind to a young mulatto from Haiti who was captured by the Americans. His name was Jean Pierre Boyer who became the president of the Republic of Haiti and later sent a present of $400 each to the widows of Consider Sterry and Diah Manning in return for their kindness to him in his captivty.

A—Samuel Manning
B—1750
C—Faces South-East
D—Wood
E—Gambrel
F—Originally stone, replaced by 2 brick chimneys
G—One story and half
I—I window each side of the two front doors; 6/6 sash
J—Stone

86 TOWN STREET
LORD TAVERN

This house stands on the Rev. James Fitch home lot. In February 1702 the Reverend Fitch and his son, Daniel, sold property to John Waterman, born 1672, son of Lieut. Thomas and Miriam (Tracy) Waterman. After his death, the widow and her son transferred the property in 1755 to Nathaniel Backus, Jr., husband of Elizabeth Waterman. He sold it to Eleazer Lord, Sr., who in turn deeded it to Eleazer Lord, Jr., in 1760. This one acre is the corner at 86 Town Street. There is no mention of a house standing on the lot at that time and Eleazer, Jr., built the present house, circa 1760. Family tradition says that it was built in 40 days.

Eleazer Lord, Jr., was born about 1729 and in 1735 he married his cousin, Elizabeth Lord. They had two daughters.

In this house Mr. Lord kept an Inn which was frequented by lawyers attending the sessions at the Court of Norwich which was located across the street. In 1809 he died and left the property and home to his family. The house is often called the Compass House because it faces due north. The ell of the building has served as the Norwichtown post office at various times.

A—Eleazer Lord, Jr.
B—1760 (Source: Perkins)
C—Faces North
D—Wood
E—Peak
F—Brick, central
G—Two stories and a half
H—On South-west side: 2 story ell on South side
I—7 windows front; 2 windows right and 1 left of door; new 2/2 sash
J—Stone
K—Interior altered somewhat; chimneys have been rebuilt.

44 EAST TOWN STREET
TRUMBULL-CAREW HOUSE

Capt. Joseph Carew, son of Joseph and Mary (Huntington) Carew, was born in 1738. In 1765 he married Eunice, daughter of John and Phoebe Edgerton. He was a carpenter by trade and later became a retail merchant and owned a shop purchased from Zachariah Huntington. He temporarily gave up his business in 1781 to serve as a Captain in a company at West Point. In 1793 he and his son-in-law, Joseph Huntington, entered business together as Carew and Huntington.

Col. Joseph Trumbull purchased this property from Carew in 1778. He was the son of Governor Jonathan and Faith (Robinson) Trumbull of Lebanon. He was born in 1737 and educated at the Tisdale School in Lebanon and graduated from Harvard in 1756. He then went into the business of his father known as Trumble, Fitch and Trumble.

In 1775 he was appointed first Commissary General of the American Army, an office of great responsibility which overtaxed his health. Although feeling poorly, he married Amelia Dyer of Windham in 1777. He died at his father's residence in Lebanon in 1778.

A—Capt. Joseph Carew
B—1763
C—Faces North
D—Wood
E—Peak
F—1, late brick
G—Two stories and a half
I—5 windows f r o n t, half house, paired 2 windows right of corner door; 3 on second floor; 6/6 sash
J—Stone
K—Exterior remodeled about 1840

40 EAST TOWN STREET
ENTRANCE TO THE OLD BURYING
GROUND

The old burying ground at the end of the Old Cemetery Lane was purchased in 1699 and in 1796 an addition was acquired. The gates shown here were placed at the entrance to the latter purchase.

The gates are called the Amos Hallum Hubbard Gates and were acquired from the Palmer Smith estate by the Daughters of the American Revolution. They were dedicated on July 5, 1903. Originally the gates guarded the entrance to the Amos Hallum Hubbard Mansion, built in 1832. The Mansion was torn down in 1903 to make way for the present Post Office on Main Street in downtown Norwich.

The iron from which these gates were molded is supposed to have come from the famous Salisbury Iron Mines in Litchfield County, Connecticut. The Salisbury Mines produced iron for Revolutionary War cannons, cannon balls, the anchors for the frigate *Constitution* ("Old Ironsides"), and the chain that blockaded the Hudson River.

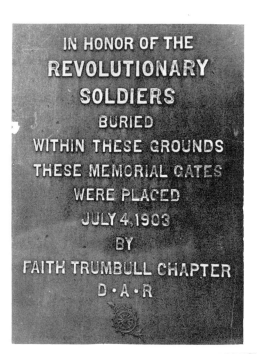

IN HONOR OF THE
**REVOLUTIONARY
SOLDIERS**
BURIED
WITHIN THESE GROUNDS
THESE MEMORIAL GATES
WERE PLACED
JULY 4, 1903
BY
FAITH TRUMBULL CHAPTER
D·A·R

BRONZE TABLETS
AT THE ENTRANCE
TO THE BURIAL
GROUNDS

**REVOLUTIONARY SOLDIERS
BURIED IN THIS CEMETERY**

CAPT. ISAAC ABEL — CAPT. JAMES HYDE
LIEUT. RUFUS BACKUS ABEL — THEODORE HYDE
CAPT. ELIJAH BACKUS — DRUMMER PARMENAS JONES
CORP. EZEKIEL BARRETT — ENSIGN AZARIAH LATHROP
SERG. ZEPHANIAH BLISS — DARIUS LATHROP
ELIPHALET CAREW — JEDIDIAH LATHROP
CAPT. JOSEPH CAREW — JONATHAN LATHROP
PAY'R GARDNER CARPENTER — ZACHARIAH LATHROP
SERG. NATHAN CHAPEL JR. — ANDREW LEFFINGWELL
EDWARD CONDY — COL. CHRIST. LEFFINGWELL
COL. JOHN DURKEE — LIEUT. DANIEL LEFFINGWELL
CAPT. ELISHA EDGERTON — ENSIGN ELISHA LEFFINGWELL
CAPT. JOHN FANNING — JOHN LEFFINGWELL
THOMAS FANNING — PHINEAS LEFFINGWELL
STEPHEN GIFFORD — CAPT. SAMUEL LEFFINGWELL
CAPT. SILAS GOODELL — DRUMMER DIAH MANNING
ABEL GRISWOLD — CAPT. BELA PECK
LIEUT. ANDREW GRISWOLD — CAPT. JOSHUA PENDLETON
COMM'Y ANDREW HUNTINGTON — DR. DAVID ROGERS
BENJAMIN HUNTINGTON — COL. ZABDIEL ROGERS
SERG. CALEB HUNTINGTON — JONATHAN STARR
GEN. EBENEZER HUNTINGTON — JABEZ TRACY
GEN. JABEZ HUNTINGTON — CAPT. FREDERICK TRACY
GEN. JEDIDIAH HUNTINGTON — DR. PHILEMON TRACY
SERG. JOHN HUNTINGTON — URIAH TRACY
LIEUT.-COL. JOSHUA HUNTINGTON — SIMEON THOMAS
GOV. SAMUEL HUNTINGTON — CAPT. ASA WATERMAN
CAPT. SIMEON HUNTINGTON — CAPT. NEHEMIAH WATERMAN
ARIEL HYDE — ASA WOODWORTH
CORP. JOSHUA YEOMANS

THESE NAMES
WERE IDENTIFIED BY
GEORGE SHEPARD PORTER

[29]

34 EAST TOWN STREET
GOVERNOR SAMUEL HUNTINGTON
HOUSE

Governor Samuel Huntington was one of the most distinguished citizens of Norwich. Born on July 3, 1732 in Scotland, Connecticut, he was the eldest child and as a boy was a farmer. Through self education and perseverance he became a distinguished lawyer.

In 1760 he moved to Norwich and in 1761 married Martha, daughter of the Reverend Ebenezer Devotion of Windham. They had no children of their own but adopted two children of his brother, Rev. Joseph Huntington, who also had married a Devotion girl.

In 1764 Samuel Huntington became a representative of the Town of Norwich to the General Assembly. In 1774 he was appointed Associate Judge in Superior Court and in 1775 became a member of the Council of Safety of Connecticut and was appointed delegate to Congress. He was seated in the Continental Congress in 1776 and became one of the Signers of the Declaration of Independence. He was elected President of the Continental Congress in 1779 and served in that capacity until July, 1781. He became Chief Justice of the State of Connecticut in

A—Governor Samuel Huntington
B—1783
C—Faces North
D—Wood
E—Peak
F—2 brick, at ends
G—Two stories and a half
H—Large, 2 story ell on South side
I—Originally 9 windows front, paned, 1/1 sash. Window above changed to door. Raised paneled caps; triangular in shape over first floor windows.
J—Stone
K—The large clapboarded structure has been extensively remodeled. Only the central dwelling with the corner pilasters is original. The following features are all modern: Two square railed panels each side of front door with leaded glass strips above fluted pilasters which outline door opening. Large open porch with four round supporting columns and gabled roof in center front of house.

1784, and in 1785 was elected Lieutenant Governor. In 1786 he became Governor and held the position for ten years. He died in 1796.

This building is now being used as the offices of the United Workers of Norwich, the organized charities of Norwich. The physical building has been extensively altered over the years.

23 EAST TOWN STREET
GENERAL JEDEDIAH HUNTINGTON
HOUSE

General Jedediah Huntington was born in 1743, the son of General Jabez and Elizabeth (Backus) Huntington. He graduated from Harvard College with honors, and then went into business with his father. He became a valiant soldier during the Revolution and fought courageously during the Battle of Bunker Hill, from which he emerged a Colonel.

After the Battle of Bunker Hill he fought in New York and Pennsylvania. He endured the hardships of Valley Forge and helped repulse the British at Danbury, Connecticut, in 1776. In 1777, at General Washington's request, he was made a Brigadier General and at the end of the war received the commission of Major General. After the war he served many important positions such as High Sheriff for the County of New London, Judge of Probate for the district of Norwich, First Alderman of the city of Norwich, one of the representatives of the town in the State Legislature. He was one of the founders of the Order of Cincinnati.

A—General Jedediah Huntington
B—1765
C—South-west
D—Wood
E—Gambrel
F—2 central, stone
G—Three stories
I—9 window front, 6/6 sash, "Bricked" caps, the center one higher and flaring at the top.
J—Stone
K—Overhung gable at third floor level

MARKER ON EGG-SHAPED GLACIAL BOULDER FOUND
ON JEDEDIAH HUNTINGTON HOME LOT

He married Faith Trumbull in 1766, daughter of Governor Jonathan Trumbull of Lebanon, Connecticut. They had one son, Jabez. After her death he married Ann Moore of New York. They had seven children.

General Jedediah Huntington was the first collector of U. S. Customs under the Federal Constitution. He was appointed in 1789 by General Washington, removed to New London and built a home there at the corner of Broad and Washington Streets. He died in New London in 1818 at the age of 75. He was initially buried in New London but his remains were later removed to Norwich and buried in the old burying grounds near the Green.

This house contains a very handsome staircase with mahogany rail and rope balusters.

19 EAST TOWN STREET
HUNTINGTON-LATHROP HOUSE

In 1738 Jabez Lathrop, grandson of Samuel Lathrop, sold his share of his grandfather's homelot with house, barn, cider press and mill to Captain Joshua Huntington. We cannot be positive that this house is the old Lathrop Mansion but according to record a large price was paid for the property and we can assume that Joshua either altered or remodeled the old house since it has many features which indicate an origin earlier than 1740. Joshua moved to the Lathrop lot and gave to his son, Jabez, his former homestead on the Bradford land—now 16 Huntington Lane.

Joshua was born in 1698 and in 1718 married Hannah, daughter of Jabez and Hannah (Lathrop) Perkins. He was a noted merchant, beginning business and pursuing it for 27 years. He was one of the first to start the new settlement at the Landing and received a grant of land, 20 feet square, on the west side of Rocky Point.

He was the highest on the list of subscribers to the Norwich-Preston Bridge built over the Shetucket River in 1737. He died of yellow fever August 27, 1745.

A—Capt. Joshua Huntington
B—1738 or remodeled earlier building
D—Wood
E—Peak
F—End—2 both new and moved to the ends
G—Two and a half stories
I—French windows added since alterations
J—Stone
K—Extensively remodeled interior and exterior; peak on front added since 1895.

25 SCOTLAND ROAD
THOMAS DANFORTH HOUSE

Thomas Danforth was born in 1703, a descendant of an old and distinguished Massachusetts family. His father was the Rev. Samuel Danforth, 2nd, who for 44 years was the Pastor of the Church at Taunton, Massachusetts.

He was the first pewterer in the Danforth family. Examples of his work are on exhibit at the Metropolitan Museum of Art, the New Haven Colony Historical Society and at the Leffingwell Inn in Norwich.

Thomas Danforth I of Taunton, Mass., and Norwich, Conn., and his descendants (including the Boardmans) and their trainees were predominant in the pewter trade for nearly a century. (Guide to American Pewter by Carl Jacobs.)

Scotland Road, the site of this house, was known as Danforth Road for many years.

A—Thomas Danforth
B—1746
C—Faces South
D—Wood
E—Peak
F—1 stone, central
G—One story and a half
H—Recent addition on North east end
I—2 windows west of front door; 1 above door, 2/2 sash
J—Stone
K—Exterior: changed. Porch has been built over front door. Doorway to East of center at end. Interior: Heavy beams show adze marks. Only one fireplace in south-west room, has a heavy stone lintel with date "1746" inscribed.

30 HUNTINGTON LANE
REV. JOSEPH STRONG HOUSE

Joseph Strong, son of Rev. Nathan Strong of Coventry, Connecticut, was born September 21, 1753. He graduated from Yale College at the age of nineteen. He returned to Yale after graduation and reviewed many of his studies and afterward prepared for the ministry.

He was first called to the First Congregational Church in Norwich as a colleague of the Rev. Dr. Lord where he was ordained in 1778, the charge being given by his father. He remained Pastor of this Church until his death December 18, 1834. It is reported that his sermons were direct, simple and very earnest.

His marriage to Mary Huntington on October 8, 1780, daughter of Jabez and Hannah Huntington, gave them title to the land where this house was built for the young couple.

He was a member of the Corporation of Yale College for 18 years.

A—Rev. Joseph Strong
B—1778
C—Faces South
D—Gambrel
F—2 central
G—Two stories and a half
H—Ell: 2 story ell at east end
I—Originally 9 window front
—6/6 sash
J—Stone
K—Restored, original; interior, no paneling

11 HUNTINGTON LANE
COLONEL JOSHUA HUNTINGTON
HOUSE

Joshua Huntington was born in 1751, son of General Jabez and Hannah (Williams) Huntington. In 1771 he married Hannah, the daughter of Colonel Hezekiah Huntington.

At the beginning of the Revolution he was already well established in a prosperous business at the Landing, had vessels of his own, and had served as Lieutenant of the militia. Although he felt that his business claims required his presence at home, he remained with the Army and served for some time in New York. He was discharged with the rank of Lieut. Colonel.

He was later engaged in securing ships for the service and in fitting our privateers. He was agent for Wadsworth & Carter of Hartford in supplying the French Army at Newport with provisions and had charge of the prizes sent by the French Navy to Connecticut.

Hannah died in 1815 and Joshua died in 1821.

A—Col. Joshua Huntington
B—1771
C—West
D—Wood
E—Gambrel
F—2 brick, central
G—Two stories and half
H—2-story ell on east end
I—9 window front, 12/12 sash
J—Stone
K—Completely restored. Attractive grounds with large trees.

16 HUNTINGTON LANE
BRADFORD-HUNTINGTON HOUSE

One of the most interesting old homes to survive, this house is one of the three remaining structures built by a founder. It was built in different sections at various periods.

In 1691 Simon Huntington, Jr., purchased the land and "new dwelling house." Additions to the house were attributed to him. In 1719 Simon's son, Joshua, obtained the homestead. The heavy, plain, box cornice, the attic overhang, and the pediments over the end windows are all primitive features of the 1719 addition.

The broad rear ell along Huntington Lane was built by Joshua's son, General Jabez Huntington, a wealthy West Indian trader who came into possession of the property in 1745. He installed much of the fine paneling. Some of the shutters have heart-shaped openings, and the double door on the ell is studded with nails in diamond patterns. The interior hardware is notable. Leaden sash weights from this old house were cast into bullets during the Revolution.

A—John Bradford, 1660
  Jabez Huntington, 1705-
  1719
B—Framing prior to 1691
C—Faces South
D—Wood, clapboard
E—Gambrel
F—Stone central on 2 sections; total, 4
G—Two stories and a half
H—Porch on East side
I—9 window front, 12/12
  and 9/6 sash
J—Field stone

General Jabez Huntington was born in
1719. After graduating from college in 1741
he entered into commercial life in Norwich,
added largely to his father's ample fortune,
and at the beginning of the Revolution,
owned a large number of vessels engaged in
foreign trade. Though fully aware of the
risk to his business, he was an ardent partici-
pant in the War of Independence. He gave
largely of his fortune to the cause.

General Jedediah Huntington was one of
their sons, born August 4, 1743. In 1741-2
he married Elizabeth, daughter of Samuel
and Elizabeth (Tracy) Backus. She died in
1745. He then married Hannah, daughter of
the Reverend Ebenezer Williams of Pomfret.

According to Crofut's *Guide to Historic
Sites,* George Washington spent the night of
April 8, 1775 at this house. Lafayette is said to
have been entertained here during some of his
visits to Norwich.

2 CANTERBURY TURNPIKE
SAMUEL AVERY and MAJOR THOMAS
TRACY HOUSE

This property was part of the Thomas Slu-man home lot of 1663. Samuel Avery and Major Thomas Tracy opened a mercantile business in a shop here in 1793. Samuel Avery was married to Candace Charlton, daughter of Richard Charlton in 1780.

Major Thomas Tracy was born in 1767 and was married to Elizabeth, daughter of Samuel Avery. Major Tracy died in 1806 before the birth of his only child, a daughter Ann. After Tracy's death, Sam Avery took his son, Henry, into partnership. The firm was then known as Samuel Avery and Son. The business was later sold and was known as Roger Huntington and Co. with Henry Avery as a partner.

In 1856 William Jackson purchased the property and shop and remodeled it into the home presently found on the lot.

A—Samuel Avery and Major Thomas Tracy
B—1785
C—Faces South
D—Wood
E—Peak
F—2 brick, central
G—Two stories and a half
H—2 story on North side, 2 story with front overhang added on East end, not quite flush with front of house.
I—6 west of the front door; 6/6 lights
J—Stone

10 OX HILL ROAD
THE MICHAEL DARROW HOUSE

Michael Darrow was a farmer who migrated to Norwich in 1743 to start a farm. He built a one-room house in which he lived when not traveling to and from New London.

In 1773 there is record of admission of this family to the town as dwellers and we can assume that this is the time the present house was built. It is not known if he incorporated the one-room house into the present dwelling.

Clarence Darrow, the famous lawyer, was a direct descendant of this Michael Darrow.

A—Michael Darrow
B—1743-1773
C—Faces South-west
D—Wood
E—Peak
F—1 brick, central
G—Story and a half
H—Main house has ell which also has an ell extending to the old Jail
I—6/6 sash, one window each side of door. 4 lights over door transom
J—Stone
K—Restored

425 WASHINGTON STREET
DANIEL TRACY HOUSE

Daniel Tracy was born in 1756, the son of Josiah and Rachael (Allen) Tracy. They had eight children. Rachael died 1761. Daniel married Esther Richard Pride in 1783 and they had two children.

He was a house carpenter by trade and built this lovely home in 1785. Then he moved to Newton, Massachusetts, and later Dover, New Hampshire. In 1798 Stephen Backus from Brooklyn, Connecticut, bought the home. After a succession of owners, Charles Bliss bought the house in 1839, whose heirs later sold it to George Rudd, who generally modernized the house.

A—Daniel Tracy
B—1785
C—Faces West
D—Wood
E—Peak
F—Stone, central
G—Two stories and a half
I—9 window front, new 6/6 sash
J—Stone
K—Restored.

410 WASHINGTON STREET
CHRISTOPHER HUNTINGTON, JR.,
HOUSE

Christopher Huntington, 2nd, or Deacon Christopher as he was frequently referred to, was born November 1, 1660, and was the first male child born in Norwich. He was the son of Christopher and Ruth (Rockwell) Huntington. In 1681 he married Sarah, daughter of Thomas Adgate. She died in 1705-06 and he then married Mrs. Judith (Stevens) Brewster, the widow of Jonathan Brewster.

Christopher was a deputy and frequently chosen as a townsman. He served as town clerk, succeeding Richard Bushnell from 1698 to 1702. He was an expert surveyor and frequently settled questions of boundary. He was appointed a deacon in 1695-6.

He had a total of eleven children. He died in 1735 and the property was inherited by sons, John and Jeremiah. John subsequently deeded his portion of the properties to Jeremiah and when he left Norwich, he sold the property to Samuel Avery.

A—Christopher Huntington, Jr.
B—Prior to 1735
C—Faces East
D—Wood
E—Peak
F—1 stone & brick, central behind ridge
G—Two stories and a half
H—On West end
I—2 windows right of door and 1 left; 6/6 sash
J—Stone
K—Interior: Original. Exterior: Porch on South side. Well-kept grounds enclosed with white picket fence. Gardens on the South and West of house.

[43]

409 WASHINGTON STREET
JAMES NORMAN HOUSE

This is the site of the Isaac Huntington blacksmith shop. In 1722 Christopher Huntington sold this property to James Norman. He either altered the shop into a dwelling or built this home on the site.

Mr. Norman is probably a descendant of the Massachusetts Norman family. He married Mary (Rudd) Leffingwell, widow of Nathaniel Leffingwell, and daughter of Jonathan and Mercy (Bushnell) Rudd. They had three children.

He was, among other things, a ship captain engaged in trade with the Barbados. While in Norwich he was also a mercantile shopkeeper and in 1717 was licensed to keep an inn. His son, Joshua inherited the home.

The house is situated on a bank up from the street, with a basement in the rear and to the west side. In front of the house on the south side is a walled garden.

A—James Norman
B—1760
C—Faces West
D—Wood
E—Gambrel
F—1 brick, central
G—Story and a half
I—6/6 sash
J—Stone
K—Interior: Remodeled. Exterior: Original.

407 WASHINGTON STREET
JOSHUA PRIOR HOUSE

Joshua Prior built this home about 1766 at the time of his marriage to Sarah Hutchins of Killingly and resided here for several years. In 1790 he sold it to Gideon Birchard.

Birchard was born in 1735, the son of John and Jane (Hyde) Birchard and was the great-grandson of John Birchard, the first town clerk of Norwich. He was a carpenter by trade. In 1757 he married Eunice Abel, daughter of Capt. Joshua and Jerusha (Frank) Abel and they had eight children.

The splendid doorway has fluted pilasters with rosettes carved above molded top and gabled point broken at the center with a block central motif. Six-paneled raised double front door.

A—Joshua Prior
B—1766
C—Faces West
D—Wood
E—Peak
F—1 central brick
G—Two stories and a half
H—2 story on East side
I—9 window front; 6/6 sash
J—Squared stone
K—Original

[45]

382 *WASHINGTON STREET*
LOWTHORPE MEADOWS

This plot of land, now known as the Lowthorpe Meadows, was deeded in 1905 to Wallace S. Allis, Caroline T. Gilman, Elizabeth Gilman, George H. Gilman, Charlotte C. Gulliver, William H. Palmer and Herbert L. Yerrington. The deed reads as follows:

Dear Friends,

For the consideration of the love and good will that we have to the inhabitants of the town of Norwich, we desire to give to you and your successors for ever the greater part of the land owned by us on the west side of Washington Street, as shown by the accompanying plan, that it may be kept perpetually as a free open space for the public good, unincumbered by dwelling houses, barns or any nuisance whatever.

Emily S. Gilman
Louisa G. Lane
Norwich, Conn. Nov. 30, 1905

The name Lowthorpe comes from the old English form of Lothrop or Lathrop. In 1745, Thomas Lathrop owned this property. This same Thomas Lathrop was an ancestor of the Gilman family.

GATE TO
LOWTHORPE MEADOWS

*   *   *

A NOTE ON BENEDICT ARNOLD

Benedict Arnold came from an excellent family background. His grandfather was Governor of Rhode Island. His mother was the daughter of a prominent citizen and her epitaph states that "she was a pattern of piety, patience and virtue."

As a soldier Benedict Arnold was fearless, a brilliant leader in battle, at his best in a hot fight, an able strategist and a great general. General Washington had great respect for his competence in military matters. At the battle of Saratoga, October 7, 1777, he led a fierce assault that repulsed Burgoyne and was wounded in the leg.

If he had died at that point, he would be counted one of our country's great heroes. But resentments, overweening ambition, vanity and greed led him to commit traitorous acts. He was extravagant, irascible and untrustworthy and in private life was always in legal trouble because of sharp practices.

The only remaining evidence of the Arnold Homestead is the Benedict Arnold Well at 299 Washington Street.

385 *WASHINGTON STREET*
THOMAS LATHROP HOUSE

Thomas Lathrop, son of Dr. Joshua Lathrop, was born in 1762. In 1783 he married Lydia, daughter of Captain William and Lydia (Coit) Hubbard. She died in 1790 and in 1791 he married Hannah, daughter of Captain Ephraim and Lydia (Huntington) Bill.

He went into partnership with his father, Dr. Joshua Lathrop, in the Apothecary Shop and later entered into a partnership with his cousin, Daniel Lathrop Coit, until his retirement.

The house reflects the personality of Thomas Lathrop. It was referred to as "the elegant mansion" admired by the townspeople of his day. Thomas Lathrop died in 1817.

The portico on the front of the house has been added since 1895.

A—Thomas Lathrop
B—1783
C—Faces West
D—Wood
E—Peak
F—2 stone, central
G—Two stories and a half
I—9 window front; 6/6 sash
J—Stone
  Overhand at second story
  end

380 *WASHINGTON STREET*
OLMSTEAD-LATHROP HOUSE

This site is the John Olmstead home lot, later the Samuel Lathrop home lot, inherited by Daniel Lathrop, Samuel's son, in 1774. The original home was burned in February 1745. Recent restoration disclosed charred lumber, indicating that the original house forms part of the present structure.

Dr. Daniel Lathrop was the son of Thomas and Lydia (Abel) Lathrop. He was born in 1712 and 1744 married Jerusha Talcott, daughter of Governor Joseph and Abigail (Clarke) Talcott of Hartford. In 1733 he graduated from Yale and went to Europe to study "Chirurgery," but started the first apothecary shop between Boston and New York. Dr. Daniel died in 1782.

This house was the home of many famous persons including Lydia Huntley Sigourney, poetess, born here in 1791; Daniel Coit Gilman (1831-1908), noted educator; John Olmstead, first physician in Norwich, and Samuel Lathrop, early settler.

A—Dr. John Olmstead, Dr. Daniel Lathrop
B—1660-1745
C—East
D—Wood
E—Gambrel
F—4, brick
G—Two stories and a half
H—2 story ell to North
I—9 window front; paired, 9/9 sash
J—Stone
K—Restored, decorated in red brick color

377 *WASHINGTON STREET*
DR. JOSHUA LATHROP HOUSE

Dr. Joshua Lathrop, the son of Thomas and Lydia (Abel) Lathrop, was born in 1723. In 1748 he married Hannah Gardiner, daughter of David and Rachel (Schellinx) Gardiner of Gardiner's Island. She died in 1760 and in 1761 he married Mercy Eels, daughter of Rev. Nathaniel and Mercy (Cushing) Eels of Stonington.

He graduated from Yale in 1743 and joined his brother, Dr. Daniel Lathrop, in the first drug store in Connecticut and actually the first one between Boston and New York.

Notes: This house was built in two main parts, a saltbox section and a three-bay Georgian section. It is believed the saltbox section was the first part built. Interesting features: Original fireplaces, including a nine-foot cooking fireplace; original panelling—most in good condition; a smoking chamber in the attic and a cold storage chamber in the cellar (both built into the chimney), also an attached woodshed.

According to legend, Benedict Arnold was apprenticed to Drs. Joshua and Daniel Lathrop, and resided here at various times.

A—Dr. Joshua Lathrop
B—1763
C—Faces West
D—Wood
E—Hip
F—Brick, central
G—Two stories and a half
H—Small, with roof sloping to south built on southeast end
I—7 window front; 6/6 sash
J—Stone
K—Original condition—restored

[50]

A—Inhabitants of East School
District
B—1789 (Source: Perkins)
C—Faces West
D—Brick
E—Gambrel
F—1 brick, east end
G—Story and a half
I—2 windows on sides and 2
on ends—old 12:12 sash
J—Stone
K—Original, however t h i s
building has not been used
for many years. There is a
small entrance on the south-
east side.

365 WASHINGTON STREET
EAST DISTRICT SCHOOL

The exact date on this building is not known but it is probably late 18th century. Lydia Huntley Sigourney recalls attending school there as a four-year-old.

In 1798 Consider Sterry opened an evening school for instruction in writing and bookkeeping. He also taught mathematics, surveying without plotting, and laying out of lands. He taught sea-going men to obtain longitude at sea by lunar observations and how to find latitude by sun's altitude. The only prerequisite for these courses was that the person be able to read.

Besides his work on lunar observations he and his brother published a book on mathematics with Nathan Daboll. He edited a system of practical navigation entitled "The Seaman's Universal Daily Assistant" nearly 300 pages long. He also wrote several small treatises and political articles. All of this was attained with no training as he was completely self-taught.

Consider Sterry was born in 1761 and was the brother of Rev. John Sterry. In 1780 he married Sabra Park, daughter of Silas and Sarah (Ayer) Park of Preston. This wife died in 1794 and he married Mary (Norman) Hazen, a widow. He had 17 children.

363 WASHINGTON STREET
THOMAS WILLIAMS HOUSE

Which Thomas Williams this is, is not exactly known. It is generally believed, however, that he was from Montville. He was born in 1735, the son of Ebenezer and Hannah (Bacon) Williams. In 1767 he married Jerusha Abel.

He was a tailor by trade and had a tailor shop located on this property. He also manufactured flour of mustard at one time. In 1798 he sold his property to William Beard of Preston and left Norwich.

A—Thomas Williams
B—1759 (Source: Perkins)
C—Faces West
D—Wood
E—Peak
F—1 brick, central
G—Two stories and half
H—1 story ell on southeast end with end chimney
I—2 windows south of front door, 4 windows north; old 9/6 sash
J—Stone
K—Original condition, essentially

357 *WASHINGTON STREET*
THOMAS HARLAND HOUSE

Thomas Harland was born in 1735 in London, England. He migrated to Boston in 1773 on the same ship from which the tea was thrown overboard during the Boston Tea Party, and came to Norwich in the same year. He married Hannah Clark in 1779, the daughter of Elisha and Hannah (Leffingwell) Clark. This couple had seven children.

Thomas Harland was the finest of early Connecticut clockmakers, "a mechanician of great skill and efficiency." He made all types of clocks—spring, musical and plain clocks with brass works and a 40-inch pendulum that would swing every second. Sometimes these clocks were hung without cases and were called wag-on-the-wall clocks.

He was also known as a silversmith. An interesting side note is that he also made an early fire engine for Norwich in 1788. He copied a plan and supervised the building of the machine. His shop was located on Town Street near the Butts Lane area.

One of Harland's grandfather clocks now stands in the George Washington Breakfast Room of the Leffingwell Inn as it did when commissioned by Christopher Leffingwell some 175 years ago.

A—Thomas Harland
B—1779
D—Wood
E—Originally gambrel roof, now mansard
F—2 brick, end
G—Two stories and half
I—9 windows front; 2/2 sash; 2 windows each side in third floor
J—Stone
K—Remodeled many times; now contains apartments. Exterior: Wall painted dark red originally. It is set high up from the street with a high stone wall in front.

[53]

348 WASHINGTON STREET
THE LEFFINGWELL INN

Stephen Backus built the original house about 1675. In 1700 he sold the house and property to Ensign Thomas Leffingwell. In July, 1701 Thomas Leffingwell was granted permission "to keep a publicque house of entertainment for strangers." Circa 1715 he added to the Inn by moving up a separate structure and fastening it on to the Backus house.

Thomas Leffingwell married Mary Bushnell and they had nine children. Mary was a nurse and when her husband died, she allotted some of the rooms for care of the sick of the community. When Mary died, the house was deeded to their son, Benajah Leffingwell. Benajah married Joanna Christopher and they had thirteen children, one of whom, Colonel Christopher, inherited the Inn after the death of his father.

Colonel Christopher Leffingwell was an illustrious and ambitious member of the community, a pioneer in many fields. In 1766 he established the first paper mill in Connecticut. The same year he also started a stocking

A— Stephen Backus
B—1675
C—Faces East
D—Wood
E—Saltbox roof with added lean-to
F—3, brick. South leg of L-shaped house had a large central chimney. In 1760 this was broken into with additions and the two halves of the chimney are joined in the attic and then evolve through the roof as a single large chimney. The second chimney is in the north half of the east leg and the third in the rear lean-to sections of the northwest side of the house.
G—Two stories and half
I—4 each side of front door, 1 above, 6/9, 9/9, 12/12 sash throughout. Inside shutters in Tavern Room, George Washington Parlor and 1675 bedroom. In the basement museum are fragments of original diamond-

factory, the first of its kind. He also established a pottery mill at Bean Hill, a chocolate mill, a fulling mill, a clothiers shop and a dye shop.

Christopher was concerned with the injustices imposed on the Colonists by England. He was appointed in 1775 one of the Committee of Correspondence. He understood the importance of quietly securing Fort Ticonderoga with its extensive supplies of war material, and was one of those who united in supplying the funds to engage Colonel Ethan Allen and his Green Mountain Boys. General George Washington sought his assistance and that of Governor Jonathan Trumbull because he relied heavily on them for supplies and provisions for the Continental Army. Visits of consultation were held by these men at the Leffingwell Inn.

In 1784 Christopher gave land to open a new street, the present Broadway. The Inn is widely acclaimed as one of New England's finest restorations.

shaped, leaded casements from the 1675 house.

J—The rough-cut stone foundations date from the time when the house was moved by the Society to save it from destruction when the Route 2 and 32 Connector was built in 1956.

K—Completely restored under the supervision of Richard Sharpe, Architect and John Stone, Master Carpenter.

335 *WASHINGTON STREET*
LIEUTENANT THOMAS LEFFINGWELL
HOUSE

A portion of the framing of this house dates back at least to 1710 when Lieut. Thomas Leffingwell lived here.

In 1645, when Uncas was beseiged by the Narragansetts at his Fort on Shantok Point, and reduced to a starving condition. Lieut. Leffingwell loaded a canoe with beef, corn and peas, and under cover of the night paddled from Saybrook into the Thames and got the whole into the fort. At dawn the Mohegans elevated a large piece of beef on a pole to show their enemies the relief they had obtained. Then the Narragansetts abandoned the siege.

Under the original cellar of this house is a slave cellar some eight feet square.

A—Lieut. Thomas Leffingwell
B—1710
C—Faces West
D—Wood frame, clapboard siding
E—Peak
F—2 chimneys, brick, near ends of house
G—2½ stories
I—9 window front, 2/2 lights
K—Slave quarters under original cellar

13 HARLAND ROAD
DANIEL LEFFINGWELL HOUSE

"The small house just beyond the Samuel Leffingwell House is said to have been an old building which was moved here long ago, but its early history is unknown. It was standing here in the year 1800. It may have been used as an office at one time by Judge Hyde.

"Rufus Darby occupied it as a dwelling in the early part of the 19th century. It is possible that this may have been the building which Daniel Leffingwell used as a stocking factory in 1776. After Daniel's death, his father, Samuel, carried on the business. Samuel Leffingwell may have afterwards moved to the shop on Washington Street where Louis Barrel was later located."—*Old Houses of the Antient Town of Norwich.* Mary Perkins — p. 51-52.

A—Daniel Leffingwell
B—Prior to 1800
C—Faces West
D—Wood frame, clapboard siding
E—Gambrel with two dormers
F—Brick, central
G—1½ stories
H—1½ story gambrel roof wing on east
I—Most of the windows are 6/6 lights
J—Stone
K—May have been a stocking factory

276 *WASHINGTON STREET*
CAPTAIN JONATHAN CHESTER HOUSE

This house was built some time between October 25, 1754 and August 15, 1759, by Captain Jonathan Chester of Groton, Connecticut. He was the son of Jonathan and Mary (Rogers) Chester. His grandfather, Samuel Chester, who originally came from Boston, was a sea captain in New London in 1663, engaged in the West Indies Trade.

Jonathan was married at Norwich April 4, 1751 to Freelove Waterman, a descendant of Sergt. Thomas Waterman, one of the founders of Norwich. The children of this union were 1) Lucy, born 1752, married to Shubael Abbe in Windham in 1774; 2) Freelove, born 1754, wife of Capt. Simeon Huntington; 3) Jonathan, who married Esther Jenning of Windham; and 4) Eunice, who married Claudius Michel Dumont.

A—Capt. Jonathan Chester
B—1755-1759
C—Faces Northeast
D—Wood frame — clapboard siding
E—Peak
F—Brick central
G—2½ stories
H—2½ story ell
I—9-window front, 6/6 lights
J—Brick above ground
K—Door and doorway are from Thomas Bliss House

315 BROADWAY
NORTON-PECK LIBRARY
HOUSE OF LAFAYETTE SABIN FOSTER,
L.L.D.

Lafayette Foster was born in Franklin, Connecticut, on November 22, 1806. He graduated from Brown University and was admitted to the Connecticut Bar. He served as Mayor of Norwich and as Speaker of the Connecticut House of Representatives. In 1854 he was elected to the U. S. Senate and served until 1866. After the death of President Lincoln, Senator Foster was elected presiding officer of the senate to replace Andrew Johnson.

In later years he resumed his law practice in Norwich, was elected to the Connecticut General Assembly, and served on the State Supreme Court. Today his home serves as the Norwich Free Academy Library and is known as The Norton-Peck Library in honor of Henry B. Norton who left a bequest to establish a library. This was combined with the previously established Peck Library, the gift of Harriet Peck Williams in memory of her father, Capt. Bela Peck.

A—Lafayette Foster
B—1853
C—Faces West
D—Brick
E—Peak
F—Brick
G—2½ stories
H—3-story tower on front
I—Arched windows
J—Brick

A—Built through a bequest
  of William A. Slater, Ar-
  chitect Stephen C. Earle
B—1886
C—Faces Southwest
D—Brick, with sandstone
  trim
E—Hip, tall corner tower
K—Listed in the Historic
  American Building Survey
  in the Library of Congress.

108 CRESCENT STREET
SLATER MEMORIAL MUSEUM

One of the most interesting buildings on the campus of the Norwich Free Academy is The Slater Memorial Museum. It was built in 1886 through a bequest of William A. Slater, noted businessman and benefactor of Norwich, and named in honor of his father, John Fox Slater. This large Richardson brick building with sandstone trim is characteristic of the Victorian period in which it was built. Besides paintings, drawings and prints, the museum has a large collection of casts of Roman, Greek and renaissance sculpture, a collection of Indian relics and a fine selection of early American and Victorian furniture.

42 ROCKWELL STREET
DR. JOHN A. ROCKWELL HOUSE

Built in 1818 of granite quarried on the property, by Major Joseph Perkins, soldier and physician, the Rockwell House is of special interest because of the historical items on display. Dr. John A. Rockwell, a physician, lived here for many years. He was a grandson of Major Perkins and it is for him that the house is named.

To preserve the house, his daughter, Mrs. Rockwell Cole, deeded the property to the Faith Trumbull Chapter, D. A. R., and it is now maintained as a museum by that organization.

A—Joseph Perkins
B—1818
C—Faces Southeast
D—Stone (Granite)
E—Hip roof
F—2 brick (one in ell)
G—2 stories
H—Ell to East (3 stories)
I—5-window front; 6/6 lights on 2nd floor; 18 lights on 1st floor
J—Stone
K—Now D.A.R. Museum

44 ROCKWELL STREET
NATHANIEL BACKUS HOUSE

This house stood for 200 years on lower Broadway, where it was rescued from destruction by the Faith Trumbull Chapter of the Daughters of the American Revolution in 1951. Built by Nathaniel Backus in 1750, this lovely home still retains some of its original features, such as the heavy front door framed with carved rosettes and pillars.

Nathaniel Backus was a descendant of two of the founders of the town, William Backus and William Backus, Jr. Nathaniel was born on April 5, 1704. In 1726 he married Hannah Baldwin and they had seven children. According to record, Nathaniel Backus was one of the six men in Norwich who owned their own carriages prior to the Revolutionary War.

Today the Backus House is open to the public as an historical museum.

A—Nathaniel Backus
B—1750
C—Faces Southeast
D—Wood frame
E—Gable
F—2 brick
G—2½ stories
I—5-window front, 6/6 lights
J—Stone
K—Heavy front door flanked by carved pillars and rosettes

9 CHELSEA PARADE SOUTH
TEEL HOUSE

Advertised as "The Teel House—Sign of General Washington" this former hotel built in 1789 by Joseph Teel of Preston, was noted for its fine hall or assembly room, where entertainments were held and balls, lodges and clubs accommodated. An advertisement of May 29, 1794 announces the arrival at Mr. Teel's assembly room of a party of Italian rope dancers and tumblers, and the public is invited to call and see Don Porter and Clumsy, the Clown, dance a hornpipe blindfolded over fifteen eggs. . . .

After Mr. Teel's death, the hotel was continued by his son-in-law, Cyrus Bramin. In June, 1800 the hotel was transformed into a boarding and day school under the preceptorship of William Woodbridge. After several other changes, it was purchased in 1806 by Carder Hazard, a retired merchant from Newport, by whom it was sold in 1813 to General William Williams who made it his home for over fifty years.—Caulkins.

Today it serves as the residence of the principal of the Norwich Free Academy.

A—Joseph Teel of Preston
B—1789
C—Faces North
D—Brick
E—Hip, with balustrade which also surrounds the top deck
F—4 brick end
G—3 stories
H—2 story ell on rear
I—14-window front; 6/6 lights, 1st and 2nd floor 6/3 lights, 3rd floor
J—Stone

CHELSEA PARADE

"The front of the Teel House faces Chelsea Parade, formerly Williams Park. This unoccupied piece of ground had long been used by the military companies of the district as a place for military practice and regimental reviews.

"In 1797 the title was cleared of all incumbrances and claims by Joseph Perkins, Thomas Fanning and Joshua Lathrop, and deeded by them to the Town of Norwich as a park or public parade forever."—Caulkins.

According to Sarah Lester Tyler, on September 11, 1792, the 20th Regiment of Infantry was reviewed on this plain and after that it was always called "The Chelsea Parade."—*Norwich Book of Deeds* #28, Pages 367-368-369

The inscription reads:

CHELSEA PARADE
GIVEN TO THE
TOWN OF NORWICH
FOR THE USE AND PURPOSE OF
A PUBLIC PARADE OR OPEN WALK
BY
THOMAS FANNING
JOSEPH PERKINS
JOSHUA LATHROP
APRIL 5, 1797

INTERSECTION OF BROADWAY AND WASHINGTON STREET
CAPTAIN SAMUEL CHESTER REID MONUMENT
ON CHELSEA PARADE

The inscription reads:

IN MEMORY OF
CAPTAIN SAMUEL CHESTER REID
1783–1861
BORN AT NORWICH, CONNECTICUT AUGUST 25, 1783
DURING THE WAR OF 1812 COMMANDER OF THE
AMERICAN PRIVATEER GENERAL ARMSTRONG.
CAPTAIN REID PLANNED THE UNITED STATES FLAG
WHICH WAS ADOPTED BY CONGRESS IN 1818
PROVIDING FOR THIRTEEN PERMANENT STRIPES
AND FOR STARS INCREASING WITH THE
ADMISSION OF NEW STATES.
ERECTED BY EASTERN CONNECTICUT
COUNCIL BOY SCOUTS OF AMERICA AND
SAMUEL CHESTER REID MEMORIAL ASSOCIATION
DURING GEORGE WASHINGTON BICENTENARY 1932

SACHEM STREET
UNCAS MONUMENT

In 1833, the cornerstone of a monument to
Uncas, the Mohegan Chief, was laid during a
visit of President Andrew Jackson to Nor-
wich. It stands in the Royal Indian Burial
Ground on Sachem Street where only reigning
Sachems and their descendants are buried.

185 WASHINGTON STREET
CHARLES A. CONVERSE HOUSE

The original owner of this 1870 Gothic-styled house was probably Colonel Charles A. Converse, who with his wife lived in the house for many years. Colonel Converse gave the Converse Art Gallery, home of the Norwich Art School, to the Norwich Free Academy in 1906.

This interesting two-and-a-half story home is characteristic of a certain type of Victorian construction with typical interior and exterior wood details. Its notable features are the steeply pitched roofs over the main body of the house, and steeply pitched hip roof over the tower. All the roofs are covered with red and gray patterned slate.

A—Charles A. Converse
B—Circa 1870
C—Faces West
D—Wood frame, flush sheathing
E—Steep gable
F—2 brick
G—2½ stories
H—3-story tower over the entrance
I—Most of the windows in the house are double hung. 6/6 lights or 4/4 lights
J—Random ashlar
K—Gothic details. Listed in the Historic American Building Survey

157 WASHINGTON STREET
LEARNED-AIKEN HOUSE

This house was built circa 1799 by and for Ebenezer Learned, Master Carpenter. In May 1812 the property was deeded to a B. M. Ballou. In 1871 the house was purchased by Connecticut Civil War Governor William A. Buckingham for his daughter and son-in-law, General J. W. Aiken.

General Aiken enlarged the house and remodeled the interior. The Greek revival details were probably added then.

The Italian marble fireplaces in this house were possibly designed by Bulfinch. The exterior is Colonial in style, with Federal appointments.

A—Ebenezer Learned
B—Circa 1799
C—Faces West
D—Wood frame
E—Peak roof
F—2 brick end chimneys
G—2½ stories
H—Ell on rear
I—9-window front, 6/6 lights
J—Stone
K—Greek Revival portico added 1867. Listed in the Historic American Building Survey

YANTIC FALLS — YANTIC STREET

According to Frances M. Caulkins, "The Yantic Waterfall appears to have been a favorite resort of the Mohegan Indians. It was their landing place and the fishing place. It is probable that they had wigwams at intervals in the neighborhood, and that it became one of their wandering homes."

Origin of the name — "Indian Leap"

"The Narragansetts and Mohegans were rival tribes, their sachems jealous of each other, and the people ever ready to break into warfare. According to legend, during the last great battle between these two tribes in 1643, one band of Narragansetts were forced by their pursuers (The Mohegans) to the Falls edge. They plunged either unawares or with reckless impetuosity into the abyss beneath and were dashed upon the rocks."

118 WASHINGTON STREET
VERNET-LEE HOUSE

The Vernet family, from its obscure origins at Avignon, had in four talented generations, painted its way to wealth and wide recognition throughout Europe.

John Vernet fled the chaos of post-revolutionary France and eventually found his way to Martinique. There he prospered but he decided to leave and chose Norwich as his home. His marriage to a local girl, Ann Brown, daughter of Jesse Brown, caused a large stir for his aristocratic background seemed unsuited for an alliance with a boarding house keeper's daughter. Vernet built a house at a cost and in style of elegance beyond what had previously been exhibited in Norwich.

Scarcely had the Vernet family settled in their new residence when Mr. Vernet met with sudden financial reverses, which entirely changed his plans and he sold the place in 1811 to Benjamin Lee of Cambridge, Massachusetts. It was in the Lee family for sixty years. Later it was the Rectory of Christ Church. Today, it is a private residence. — Taken from the *Study of Christ Church Rectory* by Reba Estra.

A—John Vernet
B—1809
C—Faces East
D—Wood frame, clapboard siding
E Hip
F—4 brick chimneys in north and south end walls
G—2 stories
I—9-window front, 6/1 light, Palladian window over door
J—Regular ashlar
K—Elaborate exterior ornament. Listed in the Historic American Building Survey

99 *WASHINGTON STREET*
ELIZA HUNTINGTON MEMORIAL
HOME

"The original owner of this land was Elijah Lathrop. In 1807 it was transferred to his grandson, John Lathrop, who may have had this house built, although there is no house mentioned in the deed.

"The next owner was Jonathan Dodge who purchased the property in 1832. The use of Greek Revival ornament indicates the house was probably built for him. In 1836 Jedediah Huntington purchased the property with dwelling house and barn, and it remained in his family until the 1870s when he left it in his will as a home for aged women as a memorial to his wife, Eliza."—*From the Historic American Building Survey.*

A—Jonathan Dodge
B—Circa 1832
C—Faces West
D—Wood frame, clapboard siding on front, vertical siding on sides
E—Gable
F—2 brick chimneys on main house; 1 chimney on rear wing
G—2 stories
H—Rear wing, 2 story; 3 porches, each has ionic columns
I—5-window front—6/6 lights
J—Stone
K—Notable exterior. Greek Revival ornament; above front doorway is an elaborate pediment of carved and sawn pieces

92 WASHINGTON STREET
LATHROP-BREWER HOUSE

This house has an unusual history. It originally stood at the corner of Sturtevant Street and Washington Street and was built in 1780 for Elijah Lathrop on land originally owned by John Elderkin, one of the founders of the Town. In 1798 Elijah deeded the property to his son, Lynd, and he in turn sold it to Nicholas Norris of Charleston, South Carolina.

In 1806 Jesse Brown purchased the house and in 1809 sold it to his son-in-law, John Vernet (See Vernet-Lee House). Mr. Vernet then moved it to the "John Day Lot" and it was leased by Captain Edward Whiting. In 1828 Lyman Brewer purchased it and moved it to its present location at 92 Washington Street. It now serves as an apartment house.

A—Elijah Lathrop
B—Circa 1780-1784
C—Faces East
D—Wood frame, clapboard siding
E—Peak
F—Brick central, 1 brick end
G—2½ stories
H—Porch on south side
I—9-window front, 6/6 lights

2 SLATER AVENUE
JOHN F. SLATER ESTATE

This lovely home was originally the coach-man's house to the John F. Slater Estate which stood on the ridge facing Broadway between Slater Avenue and Broad Street. Built in 1850, it is a copy of a house which the Slaters saw in Normandy during a tour of Europe. The unusually steep gambrel roof, as well as the curious number of window panes—15 over 20 in each window—add to the uniqueness of this home.

William A. Slater, son of John F. Slater, was one of the original benefactors of the Backus Hospital, and the benefactor of Slater Memorial Hall built in commemoration of his father.

A—John F. Slater
B—1850
C—Faces Southeast
D—Wood frame, clapboard siding
E—Gambrel with 2 dormers
F—2 brick chimneys
G—2½ stories
I—6-window front; 15/20 downstairs; 10/10 panes in dormers
J—Brick
K—Was built as a coach-man's house

189 BROADWAY
DE WITT HOUSE—LYDIA HUNTLEY
SIGOURNEY SCHOOL

The original owner of this interesting house is unknown although it is thought to have been built in the last quarter of the 18th century. In 1812 Lydia Huntley (Lydia Sigourney, "The Sweet Singer of Hartford") and Nancy Maria Hyde conducted a school here for young ladies.

Another of the early owners was Capt. Jacob DeWitt, a prominent Norwich merchant, who married Harriet, daughter of General Jedediah Huntington and the granddaughter of Gen. Jabez Huntington. General Lafayette called on the DeWitt family here during his last visit to Norwich.

A—Captain Jacob DeWitt
B—1775-1800
C—Faces West
D—Wood frame, clapboard siding
E—Hip roof
F—2 brick
G—2 stories
I—9-window front, 6/6 lights
J—Stone
K—Fanlights over door and in pediment on roof. Listed in the Historic American Building Survey

185 BROADWAY
HEZEKIAH PERKINS HOUSE

The house was originally owned by Capt. Hezekiah Perkins who was born in Lisbon, Connecticut, on January 15, 1751. He married Sarah Fitch of Lisbon about 1783. His early life was passed upon the sea and at one time he was commander of a ship trading with France.

The Norwich Bank was chartered in 1790 and Mr. Perkins was appointed cashier and held the office till his death. He and Jabez Huntington in 1811 gave the city the land across the street, now known as the "Little Plain," for a park.

This is an example of the frame houses built in Norwich about the end of the 18th century. It is very similar to the DeWitt House—Lydia Huntley Sigourney School neighboring on the northwest, and probably built by the same builder.

A—Hezekiah Perkins
B—Circa 1775-1800
C—Faces West
D—Wood frame, clapboard siding
E—Hip roof on front
F—2 brick chimneys toward center of house
G—2½ stories
H—Gable roof on rear ell
I—9-window front. 6/6 lights
J—Rough-cut stone
K—Fanlight in pediment over front. Listed in the Historic American Building Survey

DEACON JABEZ HUNTINGTON HOUSE
181 BROADWAY

The most noted resident of this house was Deacon Jabez Huntington who was born in Lebanon, Connecticut, on September 17, 1767. After spending his boyhood with his grandfather (Governor Trumbull), he graduated from Yale in 1784. He served as Deacon of the Second Congregational Church, as a Major in the Connecticut Regiment and was President of the Norwich Savings Society. In 1811 he and Hezekiah Perkins bought the land now known as the "Little Plain" on Broadway and gave it to the city for a park.

This house was built in the last quarter of the 18th century by Thomas Coit, son of Capt. Joseph Coit of New London and brother of Dr. Daniel Lathrop Coit of Norwichtown.

A—Thomas Coit
B—Circa 1790
C—Faces West
D—Wood frame, clapboard siding
E—Gambrel, with 4 dormers
F—Brick chimney
G—3½ stories
H—Small one-story ell to south, three-story ell to rear
I—13-window front, 6/6 lights
J—Stone
K—Window over doorway has broken arch top

JOHN JOHNSON HOUSE
171 BROADWAY

The original owner of this large Greek Revival home, built in 1840, was probably John Johnson, a bachelor whose father was a president of the Norwich bank. The house was later occupied by a Doctor Linnell.

It is a two and one-half story Greek Revival frame house with typical features. Most notable is the two-story entrance portico with four fluted ionic columns and gabled roof with pediment.

A—John Johnson
B—1840
C—Faces Southwest
D—Wood frame, horizontal siding on front, clapboard siding on sides
E—Gable
F—4 brick chimneys in outside walls
G—2½ stories
H—Ell, large rear wing
I—9 windows, front, 6/6 lights
J—Regular coursed ashlar on front, brick on the sides and rear
K—Two-story high entrance portico with 4 fluted ionic columns, Greek Revival detail. Listed in the Historic American Building Survey in the Library of Congress

WOODHULL HOUSE
167 BROADWAY

Architects have ascertained the construction date of this house at about 1830. The earliest known owners were a Mr. and Mrs. Woodhull, who lived in the house for many years. Ownership then passed to the Trumbull family, then to a Doctor Kimball.

"This stately mansion, as well as the others in this area, reflect that period (the early 1800s) of Norwich life when commerce and the textile industry flourished. The prosperous merchants and shipowners built their homes in this newly developed section of town on Washington Street and Broadway."
—*Based on statement in American Thermos Company Magazine, July 1959.*

A—Woodhull Family

B—Circa 1830

C—Faces West

D—Wood frame, flush vertical siding on front, clapboards on sides and rear

E—Hip

F—3 brick, 2 in end walls of front

G—2 stories

H—2-story ell to rear

I—9-window front, 6/1 lights first floor, 6/6 lights 2nd floor

J—Random ashlar

K—Listed in the Historic American Building Survey. Wood columns support a portico with gable roof over the front of the house. The portico is two stories high and has an elaborate lighted pediment.

62 CHURCH STREET
THE GLEBE HOUSE

Built in 1768 this was the home of the Reverend John Tyler, Rector of C h r i s t Church for 54 years. He had been ordained by the Bishop of London. During the Revolution religious services were held in the house.

Reverend Tyler took part in the historic meeting of March 25, 1783 at the Glebe House in Woodbury, Connecticut, at which Samuel Seabury was selected as the first American Episcopal Bishop. The house was later occupied by William Tyler Olcott, author and astronomer, who was the great-great-grandson of the Reverend Tyler.

A—Rev. John Tyler
B—1767
C—Faces South
D—Wood frame, clapboard roof over front door
E—Peak
F—2 brick end chimneys
G—2½ stories
H—1½ lean-to on rear; small siding
I—9-window front, 6/6 lights
J—Stone

37 OAK STREET (Cemetery)
CAPTAIN EPHRAIM BILL MONUMENT

As a part of the celebraton of the 150th Anniversary of the incorporation of the City of Norwich, a tablet was placed over the graves of Captain Ephraim Bill and his wife, Lydia Huntington Bill, ancestors of President Franklin Delano Roosevelt. This tablet was erected July 1, 1934 by the Society of the Founders of Norwich, Connecticut.

37 OAK STREET (Cemetery)
CAPTAIN ROBERT NILES MONUMENT

Captain Robert Niles of Norwich was Commander of the Revolutionary War vessel, *The Spy*. He was employed by the government to carry to France an official copy of the treaty ratified with that kingdom. Of six copies dispatched by different ships, Capt. Niles' copy was the only one able to pass through the British blockade and arrived at Brest in 21 days. This treaty hastened the departure of troops and stores which France sent to the aid of the American cause.

The inscription reads:

Capt.
ROBERT NILES
A patriot who commanded
the Spy during the Revolution.
He carried the treaty to France
delivering it to
BENJ. FRANKLIN
Capt. Niles served his country
faithfully and died a Christian
in the year 1818
aged 83 years.

307 MAIN STREET
BUCKINGHAM MEMORIAL BUILDING

Buckingham Memorial was a brick home built in 1845 and was occupied for many years by William A. Buckingham who was elected Governor of Connecticut in 1858, serving during the Civil War. General U. S. Grant, visited the Governor while President and a reception was given here in his honor, to which the public was invited. Abraham Lincoln is said to have spent a night here also.

In 1909 President Taft held a public reception in the front parlor during the 250th Anniversary of the founding of Norwich. For many years it was the headquarters of the veterans of the Grand Army of the Republic. Today it stands as a memorial to all veterans as well as to Governor Buckingham.

A—Governor William A. Buckingham
B—1845
C—Faces East
D—Brick
E—Hip roof
F—Brick chimney
G—2½ stories
I—7-window front; 6/6 lights; signs cover 2 windows
J—Cement

352 MAIN STREET
JOHN FOX SLATER HOUSE
(ELKS CLUB)

An early owner of this 1827 Greek Revival home was John Fox Slater, who was born in Rhode Island March 4, 1815. He was President of the Slater Cotton Mills at Jewett City, and founder of the John F. Slater Fund ($1,000,000) for the education of Negro freedmen following the Civil War, for which he was presented a gold medal by the Congress of the United States. He was also a benefactor of the Park Congregational Church, The United Workers, and Norwich Free Academy. The Slater Memorial Museum was built in honor of Mr. Slater through a bequest of his son, William A. Slater. He died in Norwich in 1884. This brick house is one of the largest examples of Greek Revival architecture in the area.

A—John Fox Slater
B—Circa 1827
C—Faces West
D—Brick
E—Hip roof
F—4 brick chimneys on main block
G—2½ stories
H—2½ story ell in rear (new); elevated porch on front
I—9-window front; 6/9 lights first floor; 6/6 lights 2nd floor
J—Brick
K—Entrance portico has 4 two-story Corinthian columns with gable roof. Listed in the Historic American Building Survey.

NORTH MAIN STREET
FERRY MARKERS

Two bronze tablets set in boulders were placed on North Main Street in 1932 by the Society of the Founders of Norwich to mark the way to the old Ferry across the Shetucket River. One boulder is located at the corner of South Golden Street, the other is in the yard of the Norwich Public Utilities.

The inscription reads:

THIS MARKS THE WAY TO

THE OLD FERRY OVER THE

SHETUCKET RIVER MAINTAINED

BY THE TOWN FROM 1671 TO 1784

AND USED BY

GEORGE WASHINGTON

MARCH 5, 1781 ON HIS WAY TO

NEWPORT, R. I.

This tablet placed by The Society of the
Founders of Norwich, Connecticut, 1932.

ELIJAH STREET
MIANTONOMO
MEMORIAL
MONUMENT

A crude stone structure
was erected to commemo-
rate the capture near here
of Miantonomo the Great
Chief of the Narragansetts
by Uncas, Chief of the Mohegans. The Narragansetts
were hostile to the white
settlers.

371 WEST THAMES STREET
RICHARD BUSHNELL HOUSE

Richard Bushnell, son of Richard and Mary Marvin Bushnell was born in September of 1652. He came to Norwich with his step-father, Thomas Adgate. On December 7, 1672 he married Elizabeth Adgate, and probably lived in the ell of this house, which dates prior to 1690.

Richard Bushnell was one of the most noted and active men in Norwich. He performed the duties of Townsman, Constable, Schoolmaster, Poet, Deacon, Sergeant, Lieutenant and Captain, Town Agent, Town Deputy, County Clerk and Justice of the Peace. He died in 1727.

A—Richard Bushnell
B—Prior to 1690 (ell); main 1740-1750
C—Faces East
D—Wood frame, clapboard siding
E—Peak, second story overhang on south end
F—Brick on ell
G—2½ stories
H—Ell to rear, 2 story; 1 story lean-to
I—8-window front, 6/6 lights; 12/8 lights in small rear lean-to
J—Stone foundation

MANWARING ROAD
DR. IER J. MANWARING HOUSE

Dr. Ier J. Manwaring was one of Norwich's first woman medical doctors. She died at the age of eighty-five in 1957. Born in Montville, Connecticut, December 29, 1872, she was the daughter of John and Mercy (Raymond) Manwaring. Her parents moved to Norwich in 1877, taking up residence in the beautiful country estate in East Great Plain where she lived until her death.

She was educated in the Broadway School (now gone) and received her medical education in Women's Medical College in Philadelphia, Pa., from which she graduated in 1895.

In World War I, as a member of the American Women's Hospital Unit No. 1, she was decorated by the French Government for service at Chateau Thierry and Belleau Wood.

Several years ago the house was moved from its original site (where the Thames Valley Institute now stands) to Manwaring Road.

A—Unknown
B—Prior to 1792
C—Faces South
D—Wood frame
E—Mansard roof (not original)
G—2½ stories
F—Central brick
H—Rectangular portico across front; 2 stories high with 4 square columns
I—9-window front, 4/4 lights
J—Cement

574 NEW LONDON TURNPIKE (THAMES VALLEY INSTITUTE)
GREAT PLAINS BATTLE MONUMENT

In 1927 this boulder was dedicated to commemorate the Great Plains Battle in 1643, where the Mohegans defeated their old enemies, the Narragansetts, in one of the fiercest known aboriginal encounters.

The inscription reads:

NEAR THIS SPOT
ON THE
"GREAT PLAINS"
IN 1643
THE MOHEGANS DEFEATED
THE NARRAGANSETTS
IN THE MOST CONSPICUOUS
PURELY INDIAN FIGHT
RECORDED IN THE ANNALS
OF NEW ENGLAND

21 WEST TOWN STREET
JOHN D. PERKINS HOUSE

The earliest known owner of this attractive home was John D. Perkins who owned several acres of land in this vicinity in the 1800s.

It is believed to have been constructed some time between 1750 and 1800. The original house was a 2½ story building. The ell to the rear may have been added later, giving it the saltbox appearance.

A—Unknown
B—1750-1782
C—South
D—Wood
E—Saltbox
F—Central, brick and stone
G—2½ stories
H—2-story, on East end
I—4 West front door, 2 East, 9/6 lights
J—Stone

29 WEST TOWN STREET
DR. PHILIP TURNER HOUSE

This was the home lot of Dr. Philip Turner. The actual date of the original saltbox is undetermined but is believed to be prior to 1700. At the rear of this house, on the old road that circumvented Meeting House Rocks, is a foundation of what possibly was Dr. Turner's office building.

Dr. Turner was the Surgeon General of the Continental Army during the Revolutionary War, assistant surgeon of the Army at Ticonderoga and First Surgeon of the Connecticut Troops at Boston.

In 1777 Congress appointed him Director-General of the General Hospital and later made him Surgeon-General of the Eastern department, where he remained until nearly the end of the War.

He moved to New York in 1800, continued his practice and was appointed surgeon to the Staff of the United States Army.

A—Unknown
B—Prior to 1700
C—South
D—Wood
E—Saltbox, added lean-to
F—Stone, central
G—2½ stories
I—4-windows west of door;
   6/6 sash
J—Stone

79 *WEST TOWN STREET*
WILLIAM MANSFIELD HOUSE

William Mansfield married a descendant of the Hyde family, who originally received from the Indians the land on which this house stands. He was the father of thirteen children. One of his grandsons, Zebediah Mansfield, was an Episcopal clergyman, Rector at the time of his death of Grace Episcopal Church in Yantic. One of his great-grandchildren, Colonel Charles A. Converse, gave The Converse Art Gallery to Norwich Free Academy.

The original Hyde house stood a little east of this homestead. It was the birthplace in August 1660 of Elizabeth Hyde, the first child born in Norwich.—*Based on Report on the Old Houses of Norwich by Mary E. Wattles, June 22, 1912.*

A—William Mansfield
B—Prior to 1800
C—Faces West
D—Wood frame, clapboard siding
E—Gambrel roof with 3 dormers
F—Central brick
G—2½ stories
H—Porch across front
I—6-window front, 2/2 sash
J—Stone

94 WEST TOWN STREET
BENJAMIN HUNTINGTON, JR. HOUSE

Born in 1736, Benjamin Huntington, Jr. graduated from Yale (LL.D.) in 1761. He married Ann Huntington, daughter of Colonel Jabez Huntington of Windham in 1765.

During the Revolutionary War, Huntington served in many capacities. He was at one time the Director of the Battery built on Waterman's Point, he acted as an agent of the Colonies to purchase the ship *The Spy,* he supervised the construction of the fourteen-gun Brig *Defence* in 1776, and served as a member of the Continental Congress and as a Judge of the Superior Court.

From 1784 to 1796 he served as the first Mayor of Norwich. Under his administration the first Turnpike in the country opened in 1792 (The New London Turnpike). He died October 16, 1800 in Rome, New York.—From *Notes on Person and Places of Norwich 1909.*

This house is one of the few remaining saltbox types in the Norwich area. It was probably built for the above mentioned Benjamin Huntington some time in the mid-1700s.

A—Benjamin Huntington, Jr.
B—Circa 1760
C—Faces Northeast
D—Wood frame
E—Saltbox
F—Brick, central
G—2½ stories
I—8-window front
J—Stone

122 WEST TOWN STREET
ADAMS TAVERN

This small gambrel-roofed building was built as a hat shop by Aaron Cleveland, religious and political leader and great-grandfather of President Grover Cleveland. It was moved to its present location from across the road.

"The early date claimed for the hat shop, 1647, twelve years before the founding of the Town, is not confirmed by any of the architectural features. From the light framing to the scope of the room, the construction indicates it was erected about 1780."— *Connecticut American Guide Series, Federal Writers Project 1938.*

A German by the name of Adams opened a tavern in the house in the late 19th century. He used to give a bottle of wine to the first man to drive a sleigh up from the city during a snow storm. So anxious were they to get the award that one town wit is supposed to have said they came up on the first frost.

A—Aaron Cleveland
B—Circa 1780
C—Faces East
D—Wood frame
E—Gambrel roof
F—Central, brick (not original)
G—3½ stories counting basement
H—On rear
I—3 on side facing street, 2/2 lights
J—Brick
K—Second floor overhang on North side

21R CASE STREET
JOHN LEFFINGWELL HOUSE

Five years ago this lovely home was moved from 113 West Town Street to a quiet spot off Case Street by the present owners. The original owner of this restored colonial dwelling is unknown but John Leffingwell was probably an early occupant. The house dates back to the early 1700s.

A—John Leffingwell
B—Prior 1750
C—Faces east
D—Wood frame
E—Peak roof
F—Central, brick
G—2½ stories
H—1 story leanto on rear
I—9 window front, 6/6 sash (lights)
J—Stone
K—Restored

139 *STURTEVANT STREET*
RICHARD EDGERTON HOUSE

The original framing of this two-story colonial house, it is believed, dates back to the time of one of the original proprietors of the Town, Richard Edgerton. At different periods he served Norwich as Townsman and Constable. He and his wife, Mary Sylvester, had a total of nine children. He died in March, 1692.

Since the death of Richard Edgerton this house has known many names outstanding in Norwich history, such as Huntington, Carew, Backus, Baldwin, Hyde and Gifford. In 1956, after standing for almost 200 years at 140 West Town Street, it was moved to 139 Sturtevant Street to make way for the Connecticut Turnpike.—*Based on an article in Norwich Bulletin, July 1959 and History of Norwich by Frances M. Caulkins, p. 173.*

A—Richard Edgerton
B—1660 part of the framing
C—Faces East
D—Wood frame construction, clapboard siding
E—Peak roof
F—Brick, in ell
G—2½ stories
H—Ell, 1 story high to south
I—7-window front, 4/4 lights
J—Stone

The 38 Founders listed on
the Mason Monument:

East Side
Major John Mason
Rev. James Fitch
John Pease
John Tracy
John Baldwin
Jonathan Royce
John Post
Thomas Bingham
Thomas Waterman
Robert Allen

West Side
Serg't. Thos. Leffingwell
Richard Wallis
Thomas Adgate
John Olmstead
Stephen Backus
Thomas Bliss
John Reynolds
Josiah Reed
Richard Hendys
Christopher Huntington

South Side
Lieut. Thomas Tracy
Samuel Hide
William Hide
Morgan Bowers
Robert Wade
John Birchard
Simon Huntington
Stephen Giffords
John Bradford

North Side
Ensign William Backus
Francis Griswold
Nehemiah Smith
Thomas Howard
John Calkins
Hugh Calkins
Richard Edgerton
Thomas Post
John Gager

LEE AVENUE
MASON MONUMENT
POST-GAGER BURIAL GROUNDS

The street beside Adams Tavern leads south to the Post-Gager Burial Ground, laid out as a common graveyard in 1661. Many of the early settlers were buried here, but no stones remain to mark their graves.

This burial ground was purchased by the Town from the home lot of Thomas Post in December, 1661, following the death of his wife who had been interred there. Before 1693 it was enlarged by adding part of John Gager's home lot.

The Founders' Monument was erected within the enclosure in 1871 as a memorial to Major John Mason and the thirty-eight original proprietors. On the base is inscribed "Major John Mason, Born in England, Died in Norwich, Jan. 30, 1672. Aged 73." On the shaft are names of thirty-eight of the first settlers of Norwich from 1659-1660.

EBENEZER HUNTINGTON HOUSE
45 HUNTINGTON AVENUE

Ebenezer Huntington, who was born in 1692 and died in 1768 is said to have built this large house in 1717. He was one of the four sons of Deacon Simon Huntington and grandson of the first Simon Huntington. According to Caulkins, the four Huntington brothers, who were dwellers on Bean Hill, grew up to manhood in Norwich and then went away to other places. Their descendants are scattered from the Atlantic to the Pacific.

A—Ebenezer Huntington
B—Circa 1717
C—Faces Southwest
D—Wood frame, clapboard siding
E—Peak roof
F—Brick central chimney
G—2½ stories
H—Ell on rear
I—9-window front, 6/6 lights
J—Stone

46 HUNTINGTON AVENUE
CHARLES AVERY HOUSE
JONATHAN AVERY HOME LOT

This eighteenth century partial saltbox house was probably built sometime after 1752 by Charles Avery, who received the land from his father, Jonathan. He married Abigail Post in April, 1750 and their first child, Hannah, was born in January of the next year.

Jonathan Avery, on whose home lot this house stands, was a shoemaker or cordwainer by trade and had a shoe shop on the Town Street.

A—Charles Avery
B—1752-1774
C—Faces East
D—Wood frame, clapboard siding
E—Saltbox (partial)
F—Brick central
G—2½ stories
I—6-window front, 6/6 lights
J—Stone
K—Interior and exterior restored

210 WEST TOWN STREET
JOHN BALDWIN HOUSE

Part of the framing of this house is from the house which John Baldwin built on his home lot in 1660. In 1957 the house was purchased by The Southern New England Telephone Company, and was doomed for demolition so that an office building might be erected on the site. The telephone Company architect, however, discovering that some of the framing and other characteristics dated back to the eighteenth century and that its construction was added to around 1750, decided that the building should be spared on account of its historical value.

It was the home of the ancestors of two of Connecticut's Governors: Roger S. Baldwin (1844-46) and Simeon E. Baldwin (1911-15).

This 1660 home of John Baldwin, his wife, Hannah and their three children, is now the executive office of the Eastern Division of The Southern New England Telephone Company.—*Norwich Bulletin Tercentenary Edition July 1959.*

A—John Baldwin
B—Framing dates back to 1660
C—Faces North
D—Wood frame
E—Peak
F—Stone, central chimney
G—2½ stories
I—9-window front, 6/6 lights
J—Stone
K—Restored for business offices

232 WEST TOWN STREET
HUGH CALKINS HOUSE

Although the sign on this area reads "Deacon Hugh Calkins Home Lot, 1660," Miss Caulkins designates this property as the home of John Pease, a founder, from Saybrook.

She says the Calkins home lot actually was on West Town Street, south of Wawecus Street. Although it is possible that the Deacon may have lived here, it is also possible that the Hugh Calkins who lived here could have been the grandson of the first.

Hugh Calkins II was an enterprising business man who left his children a considerable estate upon his death in 1722. The description of the early resident of this house written by Bunnell Hyde in 1897 for the *Connecticut Quarterly Magazine* seems to fit this second Hugh Calkins.

A—Hugh Calkins
B—Prior to 1790
C—Faces East
D—Wood frame
E—Gambrel front, saltbox rear
F—Central, brick
G—1½ stories
I—4-window front, 4/4 lights (2 in dormers)
J—Stone

205 GIFFORD LANE
JOHN A. GIFFORD HOUSE

Walter Gifford, son of Sir Ambrose Gifford, emigrated from England to Massachusetts Bay in 1630 and was the originator of the American branch of this ancient family. The first Gifford to settle in Norwich was Stephen, one of the founders of the town. One of Stephen's sons, Samuel, married the daughter of another founder, Hugh Calkins. Their great-grandson was John Arnold Gifford, builder of this house in 1805. He was born on June 25, 1767 to Stephen Gifford of East Great Plain, who gave him this lot. John married Sally Post, who was born on April 25, 1777. They had six children. The present owner and occupant of this house is a descendant of the Gifford family, thus it has been in the Gifford family since it was built.

A—John A. Gifford
B—1805
C—Faces East
D—Wood frame, clapboard siding
E—Peak roof
F—Central brick
G—2½ stories
H—Ell to rear
I—4-window front, 9/9 lights
J—Brick above ground

FORMERLY 213 WEST TOWN STREET, NORWICH
NOW 100 CENTRE STREET, NATICK, MASSACHUSETTS
BALDWIN-SHERMAN HOUSE

It is called the Connecticut House on the Charles, and what better name for a house that was built more than two hundred years ago in old Norwichtown (Bean Hill) but sits now along the bank of the Charles River in South Natick.

In 1934 the Edward Hubbards had the eight-room house with its eight fireplaces, its ells and additions taken apart and trucked the one hundred miles to Natick, Massachusetts. Every board and timber was saved and put together on its present site at 100 Centre Street. In placing the house, Architect Hubbard turned it around so that the back of the house is now the front.

This house was the birthplace of Simeon Baldwin, well known as a lawyer, member of Congress and as a Justice of the Supreme Court of Errors, as well as a tutor at Yale. He was the ancestor of two of Connecticut's Governors—Roger Sherman Baldwin (1844-46) and Simeon Eben Baldwin (1911-1915)—Based on articles in the April 28, 1964 Boston Traveler and *The Norwich Record*, Dec. 24, 1933.

100 *TOWN STREET*
THOMAS WATERMAN HOMESITE

Thomas Waterman, nephew of John Bradford, was born in 1644 and came to Norwich in 1660. In November, 1668 he married Miriam, daughter of Thomas Tracy. They had eight children.

The original dwelling was built at a slight turn of Town Street opposite the residence of the late Dr. Turner. It projected awkwardly into the highway, which now passes over a part of the site. The old well that stood by the house is under the present street.

Thomas Waterman's granddaughter Hannah, daughter of John Waterman, married Benedict Arnold. Thomas Waterman died in 1708. The house was later destroyed.

In 1735 Nathaniel Lathrop moved to Norwich from the New London area and built a tavern on the property he purchased from Dr. Lord. It was from this tavern that the first line of coaches to Providence was started. His son, Azariah, born in 1728, succeeded his father in this business. The elder Lathrop died in 1774 at the age of 81.

Azariah was a very wealthy man and highly respected in the community. He died at the age of 82 in 1810 and left the property to his widow, and a shop to his son, Charles. In 1832 the property was sold to Bela Peck. It was shortly destroyed by fire. In 1839 the land was sold to the Union Hotel Company which erected the present brick building. It is presently being used as a home for the aged known as the Johnson Home.

86 *TOWN STREET*
HOME SITE OF REVEREND JAMES FITCH
RELIGIOUS LEADER OF THE FOUNDING FATHERS

James Fitch was born in 1622 in the town of Bocking, Essex County, England. He came to this country in 1638 at the age of sixteen and finished his theological studies under the direction of Rev. Thomas Hooker of Hartford. At Saybrook a church was organized in 1646 and James Fitch was ordained at its minister. As a pastor he was zealous and indefatigable. He trained several young men for the ministry. He labored long and valiantly in behalf of the Indians to civilize and Christianize them. He learned their language and they were warmly attached to him. In later years they gave him several grants of land; one grant consisted of 120 acres in what is now Lebanon.

When the settlement of Norwich was under consideration, the settlement at Saybrook divided sharply. Each side urged Rev. Fitch to join them and it was a hard decision for him to make whether he should stay with those who would remain in Saybrook or go with those who would remove to Norwich. He was greatly beloved and respected by all. After long deliberation he decided that it was his duty to keep with the majority, and this brought him to Norwich.

The Rev. Fitch was twice married. First in 1647 to Abigail, daughter of Rev. Henry Whitfield of Guilford, who died in 1659, and then in 1664 to Priscilla Mason, daughter of Major John Mason and Ann (Peck) Mason. He was the father of fourteen children.

In 1694 Mr. Fitch was rendered unable to preach by a stroke of palsy. In 1701 he removed to Lebanon where four of his sons had settled, and died there in 1702 in his eightieth year.

The home lots of the Rev. Fitch and Major Mason stood side by side facing the Green with the Yantic River at the rear. The road to the river (New London Turnpike) ran between the two homesteads. His house no longer stands but apparently stood about on the site of the house which at present occupies 86 Town Street.

HOME SITE OF MAJOR JOHN MASON

John Mason was born in England about 1601. He was in the Netherland Army. In 1632 Major Mason appeared at Dorchester, Massachusetts. In 1634 he was one of a committee to plan the fortification of Boston Harbor and was in charge of a battery on Castle Island. In 1635 he was a representative to the General Court from Dorchester and came to Windsor, Connecticut in 1636. In April, 1637 the Pequots attacked Wethersfield and the General Court declared war against them. An army of ninety men, under the command of Mason, sailed to Saybrook. The Pequots were established on a ridge near Groton. Mason attacked them from the rear and destroyed the Pequot tribe. He returned to Windsor.

In 1647 at the special request of the inhabitants of Saybrook, he removed from Windsor and took military command of the port at Saybrook, a position which he held for the next twelve years until he removed to Norwich.

Because of his long familiarity with Uncas and his frequent explorations of Indian country, there can be no question that he was the prime mover and ruling spirit of the undertaking to establish a new community at Norwich. It was he who negotiated the sale by Uncas of the nine miles square which became Norwich. Miss Caulkins paints the following delightful picture of an irresistible natural setting: "Undoubtedly the moving cause was to be found in the sheltered vales and fine grazing lands, the sparkling, dashing streams, the wide ranges of upland, forest and rich provisions for hunting and fishing which were included in the broad extent of the proposed township."

In 1660 he was chosen Deputy Governor of the Colony and for nearly two years performed the duties of Chief Magistrate during the absence of Governor Winthrop in England.

Major Mason was twice married; his first wife died in 1639 in Windsor. In July, 1639 he married Anne Peck, daughter of Rev. Robert Peck of Hingham, Massachusetts. They had seven children, the first of whom, Priscilla, born 1641, married the Rev. James Fitch in 1664. Mason died in 1672.

His home faced the Green to the west of the road running to the river (New London Turnpike) and was said to have been the first house erected in the new settlement. It either burned or was destroyed before 1699 for no home was mentioned on the site at that time.

Major Mason was one of the most important men in the New England area and was continually called upon in great emergencies. "He was prudent, yet enterprising; fertile in resources, prompt and heroic in the field of action . . . a fearless leader in war." (Caulkins)

THE SOCIETY OF THE FOUNDERS OF
NORWICH, CONNECTICUT, INC.

The Society of the Founders was organized October 10, 1901 and incorporated in 1956. The By-laws of the Society define, in part, the purpose for which said corporation is formed as follows:

"To perpetuate the memory and spirit of the founders or original settlers; to encourage the publication and study of the history of Norwich; to acquire and preserve documents, relics, buildings, real estate and records relating to that history."

In fulfilling these purposes the major concern of the Society in recent years has been the preservation and restoration of the Leffingwell Inn. Doomed to destruction for highway development, this historic house would have perished but for the strenuous intervention of the Society. Restored with integrity it is recognized as an outstanding accomplishment praised by all visitors including Mr. Henry F. du Pont who wrote, "The Leffingwell Inn is the last word in restoration, so beautifully presented and full of interest."

Another important contribution to the cultural life of the community was the Historical Exhibition of Norwich Craftsmen and Artists at the Converse Art Gallery September 12 through October 3, 1965. This proved to be an extraordinarily beautiful collection of rare articles reflecting the high standards of historic Norwich and its craftsmen in a revealing light. There were 221 items of Furniture, Paintings, Clocks, Silver, Pewter, Pottery and miscellaneous items loaned by museums, historical societies and individuals.

The Founders Society has a thousand members scattered through 33 states, the District of Columbia, Canada, England and Nigeria. The bond which unites this widely dispersed group is common ancestry in, and identification with, historic Norwich. It has been said, "A nation with no regard for its past will have little future worth remembering. We need authentic, tangible reminders of our national virtues and heroes to make us feel a part of the best in our heritage. If we can save enough of the homes, churches, courthouses and other places where Americans who went before us lived and worked, we can sense their way of life, their ideals and character."* This quotation expresses the convictions that inspired the restoration of the Leffingwell Inn. We believe these same sentiments actuate our far-flung membership to retain their interest in their Norwich background.

The Leffingwell Inn is most easily reached via the Connecticut Turnpike, Exit 81 East, which ends at the Inn.

The Diplomat, December, 1958.

Description of the Town Sections

YANTIC

"This section of the town retains its aboriginal name. At the time of the settlement the whole district beyond Bean Bill was called 'Yantic' . . . The name was probably derived from the syllable 'tick' or 'tuck' usually denoting, in the Indian tongue, a stream of water."—*History of Norwich,* Frances M. Caulkins.

BEAN HILL

There are several stories about the origin of the name "Bean Hill." Since there is no way to determine which of the stories is true, we include them all.

(1) "The first visitors to the spot, a group of tired and hungry prospectors, looking about them for food, found pots of beans buried in the earth."—*Reminiscences of Bean Hill,* Burrell W. Hyde.

(2) "The first planters were also famous for baked beans . . . there can be no doubt that the name Bean Hill was bestowed on a part of the town plot from the prevalence of this Saturday night treat."—Caulkins.

(3) "The area may have been suited to the raising of beans [or] may have been named for William Bean, who, in 1760, was a comrade of Daniel Boone." —*Norwich Bulletin,* July 7, 1909.

(4) "On the southwest corner of Hammer Brook Lane (Pleasant Street) and West Town Street, stood a very ancient house that dated back to the settlement of the town. Here it was, tradition says, that the people fled for safety whenever there was a report of an attack by the Indians. It was to here that on a Saturday night the people living on the hill had fled, being alarmed by the cry of 'Indians.' There were a large number of them and with but little to eat, their flight had been so hasty, that they had not time to take food with them. One family on the hill had left in their oven a huge pot of baked beans. A few men volunteered to face the danger and bring this pot of beans from the hill. It was this incident that gave the hill the name of Bean Hill."—*Recollections of Men and Things,* William T. Case.

A final note on Bean Hill: In 1833, in honor of a visit by President Andrew Jackson to the City of Norwich, it was decided by a resolution of the town fathers to change the name of Bean Hill to Jacksonville. And at one time the district was known as Westville. In spite of conflicting stories of origin and political considerations, the name Bean Hill persists.

NORWICHTOWN (TOWN PLOT)

"The oldest part of Norwich originally consisted of one long, irregular street, winding around the hills and following the course of the Yantic. It retains still the same outline, with but little variation from its first laying out."—Caulkins.

CHELSEA PARADE

According to Sarah Lester Tyler in her paper, *Norwich Early Homes and History,* "on the 11th of September, 1793, the 20th Regiment of Infantry was reviewed on this plain and after that it was always called 'The Parade'."

THAMESVILLE

"Formerly called Bushnell's Cove . . . now named for the Thames River . . . was a thriving village with an ironworks and shipyard."—Caulkins

GREENVILLE

"Was indebted in its origin to the foresight of William C. Gilman and William P. Green. The former made the purchase and the latter followed out and completed the design. It was founded upon manufacturing privileges."—Caulkins.

TAFTVILLE

This section was named for Edward P. Taft and Cyrus Taft, founders of Ponemah Mills, at one time the largest cotton mill in the world. No textile manufacturing is conducted here at present.

EAST GREAT PLAINS

The east side of the Great Plains is where the last great Indian battle took place in 1643.

TRADING COVE

Site of a trading place of the Settlers and Indians.

LITTLE PLAIN

A small park donated to the city by Deacon Jabez Huntington and Hezekiah Perkins in 1811.

Bibliography

In addition to the invaluable *History of Norwich* by Frances M. Caulkins, the following publications have provided information for this book:

The Connecticut Guide, by E. I. Hermance, Emergency Relief Commission, Hartford, 1935.

Census of Old or Distinctive Buildings in the State of Connecticut, by Elmer D. Keith, WPA, 1936-40.

Historic American Building Survey. National Park Service, Washington, D. C.

Connecticut. The American Guide Series, Federal Writers Project, Houghton, Mifflin Co., 1938.

Old Houses of the Antient Town of Norwich, Bulletin Press, 1895.

Norwich Bulletin, 1909, 1932, July 1934, July 1959.

Recollections of Men and Things, by William T. Case, 1906. This is a manuscript in the Leffingwell Inn Archives.

Old Houses and People of Norwichtown, by Mary E. Wattles, in the *Norwich Bulletin,* June 22, 1912.

Reminiscences of Bean Hill, by Burrel W. Hyde, in the *Connecticut Quarterly,* Hartford, July-December 1897.

Norwich Early Homes and History, by Sarah Lester Tyler, Faith Trumbull Chapter, D.A.R., Norwich, 1906. Pamphlet in Leffingwell Inn Archives.

Histories of Connecticut Houses. Manuscripts by Connecticut Society of Colonial Dames of America, 1914-42. Connecticut State Library, Hartford.

Index of Persons and Families

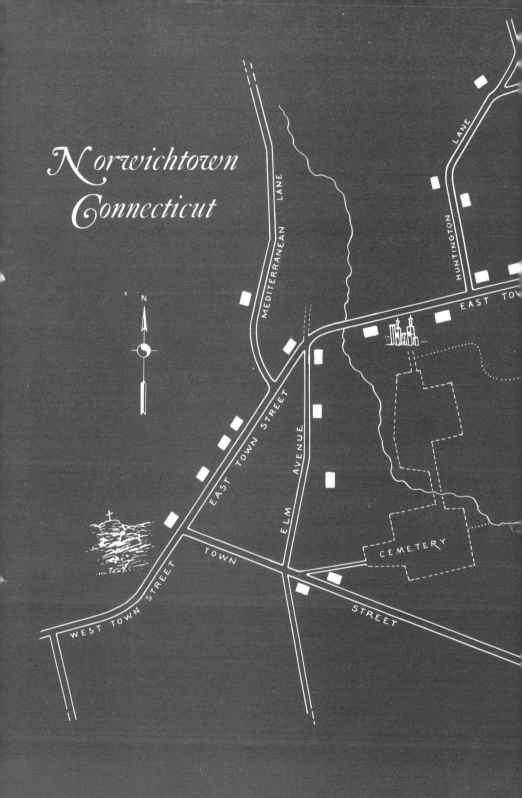

Norwichtown
Connecticut

N

MEDITERRANEAN LANE

LANE

HUNTINGTON LANE

EAST TOW

EAST TOWN STREET

ELM AVENUE

TOWN

WEST TOWN STREET

STREET

CEMETERY